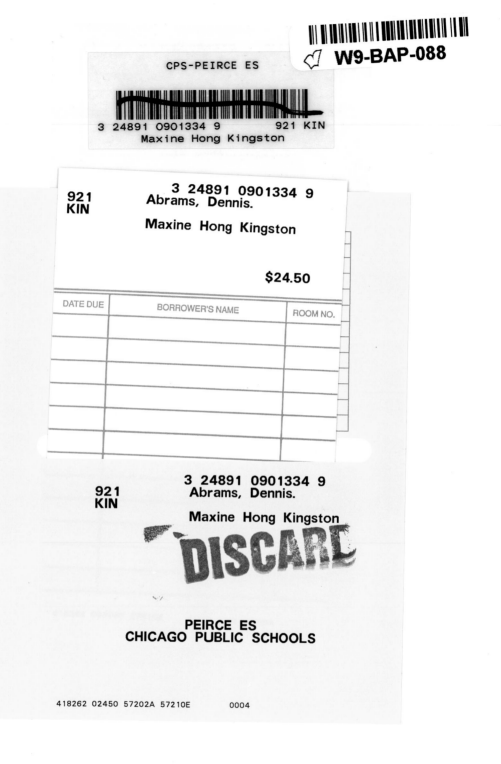

921
KIN

3 24891 0901334 9
Abrams, Dennis.

Maxine Hong Kingston

$24.50

DATE DUE	BORROWER'S NAME	ROOM NO.

921
KIN

3 24891 0901334 9
Abrams, Dennis.

Maxine Hong Kingston

DISCARD

MAXINE HONG KINGSTON

MAXINE HONG KINGSTON

DENNIS ABRAMS

CHELSEA HOUSE
PUBLISHERS
An imprint of Infobase Publishing

Maxine Hong Kingston

Chelsea House
An imprint of Infobase Publishing
132 West 31st Street
New York NY 10001

Library of Congress Cataloging-in-Publication Data

Abrams, Dennis, 1960-
  Maxine Hong Kingston / by Dennis Abrams.
      p. cm. — (Asian Americans of achievement)
  Includes bibliographical references and index.
  ISBN 978-1-60413-568-8 (hardcover)
  1. Kingston, Maxine Hong—Juvenile literature. 2. Authors, American—20th
century—Biography—Juvenile literature. 3. Asian American women authors—
Biography—Juvenile literature. 4. Chinese American women—Biography—Juvenile
literature. I. Title. II. Series.
  PS3561.I52Z26 2009
  813'.54—dc22
  [B]   2009009917

Series design by Erika K. Arroyo
Cover design by Ben Peterson and Alicia Post

Printed in the United States of America

Bang EJB 10 9 8 7 6 5 4 3 2 1

This book is printed on acid-free paper.

All links and Web addresses were checked and verified to be correct at the time of publication. Because of the dynamic nature of the Web, some addresses and links may have changed since publication and may no longer be valid.

CONTENTS

Trying to Escape

The year was 1967. The place was Berkeley, California. And Maxine Hong Kingston—wife, aspiring writer, and mother of a three-year-old son—was ready to escape the city in search of a peaceful haven in Japan.

Why did the 27-year-old high school teacher feel the need to leave? Like much of the rest of the United States, the city of Berkeley, home to the University of California, Berkeley, was in a state of upheaval. Demonstrations against the war in Vietnam, a war that many felt was illegal, unnecessary, and immoral, were growing in intensity and passion. Kingston, a longtime anti-war activist, was becoming increasingly frustrated by the war's continuance and was beginning to feel mentally and physically exhausted by the seemingly futile efforts to stop the war.

VIETNAM

U.S. involvement in the conflict in Vietnam had been going on for nearly 20 years. From 1946 to 1954, the Vietnamese people had fought to win their independence from France during what is known as the First Indochina War. At the end of this war, in which the United States had reluctantly supported the French, the country then known as French Indochina was temporarily divided into two countries. North Vietnam was controlled by the Vietnamese Communists led by Ho Chi Minh. He had led the struggle for independence, and his goal was a unified Vietnam under Communist rule. South Vietnam was controlled by non-Communists. Elections were planned for 1956 to select a government for a unified Vietnamese nation. But, because polls showed that the people would have voted for a unified Vietnam under Ho Chi Minh's rule, those elections never took place.

American policymakers believed that Communism would spread across Southeast Asia if all of Vietnam fell under Communist rule. This belief was known as the "domino theory," meaning that, if one country fell, so would the others, just like a line of dominoes. To prevent this from happening, the U.S. government worked to strengthen the South Vietnamese government. That government's oppressive policies, however, led to rebellion within South Vietnam, and the National Liberation Front (known as the Vietcong) was formed with the goal of overthrowing the unpopular government and reunifying the country with the support of forces from North Vietnam.

Early American military aid to the South Vietnamese government had largely been in an advisory role. In 1964, though, the U.S. Congress passed the Gulf of Tonkin Resolution. This bill gave the president nearly unlimited power to conduct military operations in Southeast Asia without having to ask Congress to declare war, as required by the U.S. Constitution. President Lyndon B. Johnson quickly moved to increase the number of combat troops, and by the end of 1965, more than 100,000 troops were in Vietnam.

Opposition to the war in the United States began almost as soon as the Gulf of Tonkin Resolution was approved. Initial opposition came from traditional pacifists such as the American Friends Service Committee and antinuclear activists who questioned the morality of U.S. military involvement in Vietnam. At the onset, though, most of the American public supported the war.

But as the war expanded (by 1967, 500,000 American troops were in Vietnam), so did the protests. Students and professors began to organize "teach-ins" on the war in early 1965 at colleges around the country, including the University of California, Berkeley. These teach-ins served as a forum for discussions of the war between students and faculty members. Soon, virtually every college or university had its own organized student movement, often formed under the bylaws of the Students for a Democratic Society (SDS), a leftist student-activist movement. Protests grew in size, and in 1965, the Vietnam Day Committee organized a 35-hour protest at Berkeley that attracted more than 35,000 participants.

Another important antiwar organization was the Student Nonviolent Coordinating Committee (SNCC), a civil-rights group that denounced the war as racist as early as 1965. Students and other protesters also joined The Resistance, an organization that urged its student members to refuse to register for the draft or refuse to serve if drafted. Draft cards were burned to protest a system that many believed was designed to send the poor and undereducated (college students were deferred from the draft until graduation) to die in what seemed to them to be a pointless and unjust war.

But the protests, although growing in intensity and violence across the country, seemed futile as the government continued to expand the war, despite polls that showed a growing majority of the American people opposed it. By this point, Kingston, along with her husband, Earll, had had enough of Berkeley, of its growing drug scene, and of the war itself. As she said in an interview posted on the Powell's Books Web site

More than 5,000 anti-draft demonstrators jammed Sproul Hall Plaza in October 1967 during a teach-in at the University of California, Berkeley. Maxine Hong Kingston, then a high school teacher, had been involved in the anti-Vietnam War movement for several years. By 1967, however, she was growing frustrated with the seemingly futile efforts to halt the war and with life in Berkeley.

(http://www.powells.com), "Our whole youthful culture, breaking up. . . . It was the violence of wartime. The peace movement was also becoming violent, so we were thinking that we needed to leave Berkeley."

Kingston elaborated on this in a 1977 interview with Gary Kubota for the *Hawaii Observer*:

> Things were getting really rough there [Berkeley], and we felt discouraged because, despite the protests, the war continued. A lot of our friends were also getting burned out on drugs. The tension was hard to deal with, and we thought it might be good to see what living in a different area was like. Berkeley was exciting then. People living there used to ask, "Is there life after Berkeley?" Their conclusion was no.

Of course, for Kingston, it turned out there *was* life after Berkeley. But first she would have to find out for herself exactly what that life would be.

ESCAPING BERKELEY

Some of Kingston's friends who had also "had enough" retreated from Berkeley to start communes in the woods of northern California. For Kingston, though, that was not far enough away. Her original plan had been for the family to move to Japan. On their way, they stopped off in Hawaii. Somewhat to Kingston's surprise, they ended up staying and made Hawaii their home for the next 17 years. But if Kingston thought she would be able to escape daily reminders of the war in Vietnam by living in Hawaii, she was sadly mistaken. In many ways, living in Hawaii brought the realities of the war even closer to home.

As Kingston pointed out in her essay "War," her family had not escaped from the war but had in fact put themselves right smack in the middle of it. They were as close to the war as they could be while still remaining in the United States. She wrote:

> We should have thought of it—hardware and soldiers were sent to Hawai'i, which funneled everything to

Vietnam. Tanks and jeeps in convoys maneuvered around the rim. Khaki soldiers drove khaki vehicles, camouflage that did not match the bright foliage. . . . We heard the target practice—with missiles—in the mountains, where we hiked, and looked at the jagged red dirt like wounds in the earth's green skin. . . . At the airport, near the luggage carts, we saw coffins draped with flags.

Unable to escape the war, Kingston and her husband plunged back into their antiwar activities, including counseling veterans who had gone AWOL (absent without leave). She went back to work, teaching English and language arts to high school and adult students. Most importantly, she began to sit down and write about herself, her family, and the Chinese-American experience.

Living in Hawaii gave Kingston the necessary space away from her family and her life in California to examine them more objectively. Growing up as the child of Chinese immigrants in Stockton, California, her entire life had been filled with stories of her family—of their old life in China and their new life in the United States. In Hawaii, the tranquility of the islands gave her the opportunity to think, and the natural beauty surrounding her heightened what she calls the sensory perceptions necessary for her to write. She set out to do what she had always known she would—write about her family and her life. "In a sense you could say that I was working on these books for 20 or 30 years," she said years later in an interview with Karen Horton for *Honolulu* magazine.

The resulting works, including the contemporary classics *The Woman Warrior*, *China Men*, and *Tripmaster Monkey: His Fake Book*, have made her the most critically acclaimed Asian-American writer of our time. It has been said that her work is included in more anthologies than that of any other living

Maxine Hong Kingston, whose books include the contemporary classics *The Woman Warrior* and *China Men*, is believed to be read by more college students than any other living author. Her work has led the way for a generation of Asian-American writers to find a national audience.

American writer and that she is read by more college students than any other living author. In the introduction to their collection of interviews with Kingston, editors Paul Skenazy and Tera Martin point out that "students, particularly Asian-American women, look to her as a model, find themselves in her tales. . . .

She has opened the way to a whole generation of Asian-American writers who have found a national audience for the first time."

This achievement is all the more remarkable coming from somebody who described herself as a child who "was unable to answer questions in school, who failed kindergarten, who was given an IQ score of 0 and condemned to the corner of the classroom for her so-called stupidity, and whose mother cut her tongue to improve her 'pressed-duck' voice." Through it all, though, Kingston knew that she wanted to write, that she was destined to write, that she *had* to write, telling interviewer Kay Bonetti that:

> I've never been silent.... While I've had problems speaking, I've always been a writer. There was always the wanting to tell the stories of the people coming.

And it is through the telling of the stories of the people that we learn who Maxine Hong Kingston is. Through her life and work, we will gain insight into the Chinese-American immigrant experience. We will see how the once silent girl grew up to become a teacher, an activist, and one of America's greatest living writers. Before we can learn about Kingston's life, though, we will need to learn about the world from which she came. We need to learn about modern China, about its history, about its myths, about demons, and about ghosts.

2

Where She Came From

Like any writer, like any person really, Maxine Hong Kingston is a child of her environment. She has been affected by her family, her schools, where she has lived, and by the historical and cultural events she has lived through. It is this background that lies behind all of her writing.

The experience that she and her family had as Chinese immigrants in the United States provides much of the material for her first two books, *The Woman Warrior* and *China Men*. To understand Maxine Hong Kingston and to understand *her* presentation of the immigrant experience, it is important to understand the events of modern Chinese history as well as the history of Chinese immigration to America.

NINETEENTH- AND TWENTIETH-CENTURY CHINA

Before the beginning of the nineteenth century, the nation of China had very little contact with the West. Its ties to the West began to increase in the middle of the nineteenth century, after the Treaty of Nanking ceded Hong Kong to the British and opened up five Chinese ports to British residence and trade.

Partly as a result of the Nanking Treaty, many Chinese saw their ruling dynasty, the Ch'ing, as weak and ineffective. A revolt against the government, known as the Taiping Rebellion, erupted in 1850. By the time the revolt petered out in 1864, 20 million to 30 million Chinese had died, further weakening the government and causing a breakdown in society that forced many Chinese to look elsewhere for economic opportunities.

With weakness came additional problems. In the 1890s, a war with Japan ended in a loss of Chinese sovereignty over Korea and Taiwan, and further trade and territorial rights were ceded to France, Germany, Russia, and Great Britain. To many in and out of China, the great Chinese empire seemed to be dying before their eyes.

The United States persuaded the other Western powers to recognize an "open door" policy toward China, granting all nations the right to trade with China on an equal basis. With increased Western influence in China, however, came increased anger by the Chinese against that influence. In 1900, the Boxer Rebellion broke out, with a coalition of secret societies opening a campaign of terror within China, attacking and killing Europeans and overly Westernized Chinese. A coalition of Western nations defeated this rebellion; the Chinese government by this time was just too weak to stop the rebellion on its own.

In an attempt to save itself from total collapse, the Chinese government began a series of reforms intended to modernize the country's tradition-bound system. The traditional Confucian civil-service examinations were ended (in *China Men*, Kingston describes her father attending the very last of these exams), and a more modern school system was put in place. A new army was organized, provinces were allowed to elect their own legislatures, and the government, ruled by an emperor, promised to adopt a constitution.

After their capture, three Chinese Boxer rebels were held in wooden stocks, which were connected by chains to shackles around their hands and necks. A coalition of secret societies, angered by increased Western influence in China, led the Boxer Rebellion in 1900. Western forces quashed the revolt.

These changes were too little too late. A republican movement, headed by Sun Yat-sen, led to the end of the monarchy and the establishment of the Republic of China in 1912. The country, though, remained unstable for several years until

1928, when the Nationalist Party led by Chiang Kai-shek managed to once again unite China under a single government. Just three years later, Japan occupied the Chinese region known as Manchuria and began to extend its military reach into northern China. The Asian theater of World War II had begun.

By 1945, the Japanese were defeated, but China's difficulties continued. The long war had again weakened the national government, and despite aid from the West, in 1949 it fell to the Chinese Communists, led by Mao Zedong. The Communist government, which renamed the country the People's Republic of China, tried throughout the 1950s and 1960s to revitalize the nation, so long torn apart by war and poverty, but it had limited success.

WOMEN IN THE PEOPLE'S REPUBLIC OF CHINA

While prerevolutionary China was male-centered and patriarchal, with women playing a decidedly subordinate role, attitudes changed rapidly after Mao Zedong and the Communist Party came to power in 1949. That same year, the All-China Women's Federation was founded to "represent and to protect women's rights and interests, and to promote equality between women and men." Coming after thousands of years of history that placed women in a position of inferiority, this was a monumental and historic step.

Progress has been slow and steady, and while much work remains to be done, women's lives in China have definitely improved over the last 60 years. Literacy rates for women, which in 1949 were estimated to be as low as 20 percent, had risen to 86.5 percent by 2000. And, while in 1949, women made up only 7 percent of the workforce, women today make up 45 percent of the workforce, working in educational, professional, and governmental positions. Women's health care has greatly improved, equal rights for women are enshrined into Chinese law, and opportunities for women that were nonexistent 60 years ago are readily available today.

The Cultural Revolution (1966 to 1969), an attempt by Mao to continue the revolutionary class struggle, resulted in years of chaos as nearly every aspect of Chinese life was disrupted. It was not until 1976, the year in which Kingston's *The Woman Warrior* was published and Mao Zedong died, that China began the slow path to political and economic recovery, leading to the economic powerhouse that is China today.

COMING TO AMERICA

As you can see, life in China was extraordinarily difficult throughout the nineteenth and twentieth centuries. Poverty, war, disease, and social upheaval all played a part in the desire of many Chinese to come to the United States in search of a better life. While many of them did find the new life they were seeking, they also found themselves facing unexpected discrimination and racial prejudice.

For example, many Chinese men came to America in the mid- to late 1800s to work on the transcontinental railroad, building the path and laying the tracks that joined both coasts of the country by rail line. As soon as the work was completed and the official photographs were taken, however, the Chinese workers were forced to leave, because, as Kingston said in *China Men*, "it was dangerous to stay."

Kingston goes on to explain why it was dangerous. The Chinese workers faced the possibility of torture, lynching, and murder by a hostile population that no longer needed the workers in their midst. She tells the story of her grandfather, Ah Goong, who, having worked on the railroad, would have loved the opportunity to walk along the tracks to see his work, but instead:

> Driven out, he slid down mountains, leapt across valleys and streams, crossed plains, hid sometimes with companions and often alone, and eluded bandits who

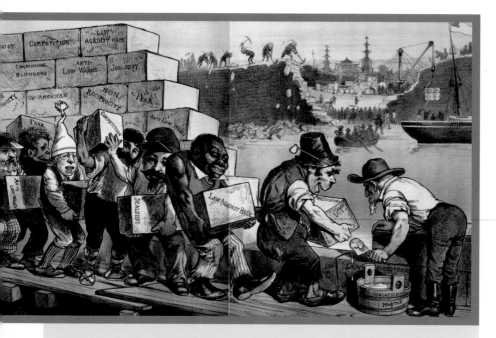

Beginning in the 1870s, the U.S. government and state governments began to enact laws against immigration by the Chinese. In this cartoon, which appeared in a March 1882 issue of *Puck*, laborers representing many ethnic groups are building a wall to exclude the Chinese. Across the sea, a ship flying the U.S. flag enters China as the Chinese knock down their own wall to permit trade.

would hold him up for his railroad pay and shoot him for practice as they shot Injuns and jackrabbits. . . . In China, bandits did not normally kill people, the booty the main thing, but here the demons killed for fun and hate. They tied pigtails to horses and dragged chinamen.

In today's America, where immigration is *still* argued about, the main topic is immigration from Mexico and the rest of Latin America. From our perspective, it's difficult to imagine that the national conversation on immigration, as well as acts of both state and national governments, was directed *against* immigration from China. But such was the case in the United States through most of the nineteenth and early twentieth centuries.

The 1870 Naturalization Act, for example, allowed only "free whites" and "African aliens" to apply for citizenship, effectively barring the Chinese. In 1878, the California Constitutional Convention drew up a constitution that denied Chinese the right to enter California. Citizens were given the power to confine Chinese already in the state to designated areas (ghettos) or to completely banish them. Chinese children were barred from attending public schools, special taxes paid only by the Chinese were enacted, and Chinese were prohibited from owning land. Employers faced the possibility of fines if they hired Chinese workers. And, amazingly enough, Chinese were not even allowed to testify against a white man in a court of law.

In 1880, the federal government signed a treaty with China limiting the number of Chinese workers who would be allowed into the country. Just one year later, this treaty was suspended for 20 years, although workers already in the country were allowed to stay and were allowed to leave and re-enter with a Certificate of Return. In 1882, Congress passed the Chinese Exclusion Act, the first in a series of laws that banned the immigration of Chinese laborers for a 10-year period. Further laws declared Certificates of Return void and directed that Chinese illegally living in the United States should serve one year of hard labor before being deported.

Not surprisingly, Chinese Americans began to fight back against the blatant discrimination, organizing the Equal Rights League and the Native Sons of the Golden State, but to little avail. The 1924 Immigration Act excluded Chinese women from entering the country and stated that any American who married a Chinese person, whether a woman or a man, would lose his or her citizenship.

The bottom line is that, throughout the first half of the twentieth century, Chinese immigration was limited to teachers, students, merchants, and diplomats. Even during World War II, when millions were being slaughtered in China, Chinese immigration to the United States was not allowed to rise. Only after the Communist takeover of China in 1949 were changes slowly made to immigration laws, making it somewhat easier for Chinese to enter the United States.

WOMEN AND IMMIGRATION

The difficulties faced by male Chinese immigrants often paled in comparison with the problems faced by Chinese women, who were long the victims of oppression in traditional Chinese society, which saw them as distinctly inferior. Immigration by Chinese women to the United States had been extremely limited, both by custom and by law.

Chinese custom said that women were required to stay behind in China while their fathers, husbands, brothers, and sons went to the United States, seen as the "Gold Mountain," to make money. For example, in 1852, of the 11,794 Chinese people in California, only 7 were women; although by the 1880s the number had increased to 1 woman for every 20 men.

As the laws against Chinese immigration tightened, the restrictions on female immigration grew even worse. From 1924 to 1930, federal law forbade Chinese women to immigrate to the United States, including the wives of Chinese men born in America who went back to China to find brides. Even when that law was revised in 1930, on average, only 60 Chinese women entered the country each year. It was not until 1952 that Chinese women could enter the United States on equal terms with Chinese men. In fact, both of Kingston's parents had illegally entered the country, a fact she was aware of and worried about throughout her childhood.

CHINATOWNS

Given these difficulties, it is not surprising that newly arrived Chinese immigrants tended to live among other Chinese immigrants, both new arrivals and those more settled. These areas, in which residents opened up businesses, restaurants, schools, and temples like the ones back in China, became known as "Chinatowns."

For those of us today who make a trip to Chinatown to enjoy a good dinner or do a little shopping, it is easy to underestimate the importance that a Chinatown had (and still has) to the Chinese. Here they were able to purchase the supplies needed to prepare traditional food. Here they were able to buy traditional clothing or see a traditional doctor dispensing time-honored herbal medicine. Here they were able to speak freely among people like themselves, enjoy traditional entertainments, and re-create for themselves a small part of the world they had left behind.

Of course, not all Chinatowns are the same. When people think of Chinatown, they generally envision something like San Francisco's Chinatown, the first and largest in the United States. This Chinatown, which served as the entryway for Chinese coming to make their fortune during the California gold rush or to work on the transcontinental railroad, is today largely a tourist destination, attracting more visitors than even the Golden Gate Bridge. (Today's Chinese immigrants in San Francisco tend to live outside the traditional Chinatown area and have settled in new Chinatowns, in the Richmond and Sunset districts.)

By contrast, in Stockton, California, where Kingston grew up, there is and was no specific geographically defined Chinatown. Instead, the Chinese community there was united, not by location, but by common rituals, traditions, and memories. And, while the Chinese immigrants who settled in San Francisco were primarily more sophisticated urban immigrants from the city of Taishan (known as the "home of overseas

Chinese immigrants in the United States recreated the world they had left behind, in urban neighborhoods known as Chinatowns. The first and largest Chinatown in the United States was in San Francisco, shown above in 1866.

Chinese"), those who settled in Stockton and the surrounding San Joaquin Valley were from a different part of China, spoke a different dialect, and were largely from small villages and farms.

Kingston described the differences in a 1978 essay, "San Francisco's Chinatown: A View of the Other Side of Arnold Genthe's Camera."

A trip from Stockton to San Francisco is a journey into foreign territory—urban, competitive, the people like

Hong Kong city slickers, not at all like the people in the San Joaquin Valley, where villager is still neighborly to villager as in the Chinese countryside they remember, helping one another, "not Chinese against Chinese like in the Big City."

OTHER INFLUENCES

There is, of course, more to Maxine Hong Kingston than being a part of the Chinese immigrant experience. She is also a product of the times she grew up in. As author Deborah L. Madsen notes in her study of Kingston, three major cultural movements defined both Kingston and the context of her work: the struggle for civil rights, opposition to the Vietnam War and the draft, and the women's liberation movement.

What these three movements had in common was a desire for social and political change that came, not from government, but from the people themselves, demanding their rights. In the case of the civil-rights movement, it was the demand that African Americans, who in the century following the end of slavery were still largely denied their rights, be finally given the same rights as all Americans: the right to vote; the right to equal treatment in hotels, restaurants, and public accommodations; the right to attend the same schools as white students.

Regarding the Vietnam War, it was, as we learned in the first chapter, the demand that the government stop fighting an unjust war and stop drafting young men to fight in it. The third of these movements, the drive for women's rights, was one that perhaps struck closest to home for Kingston.

It is said that the women's rights movement has come in two waves. The first wave, which began at the 1848 Seneca Falls Convention, culminated in 1920, when women were finally guaranteed the right to vote. The second movement, which began in the 1960s, was a broader-based movement, focusing on discrimination against women in the law and in the workplace. As a woman of Chinese descent living in the United States, Kingston strongly felt the need for women's rights, especially given the male-oriented attitude of the traditional Chinese household.

Indeed, in *The Woman Warrior*, Kingston describes the fear she had that she would be forced into a marriage, not based on love, but arranged in the traditional manner by her parents. For her, the way to escape this fate was through education, an education that would allow her to become an independent woman. In the book, she makes clear to her mother her intentions:

> Do you know what the Teacher Ghosts say about me? They say I'm smart, and I can win scholarships. I can get into colleges. I've already applied. I'm smart. I can do all kinds of things. I know how to get A's, and they say I could be a scientist or a mathematician if I want. I can make a living and take care of myself.

It is this Maxine Hong Kingston, torn between her family's traditional Chinese past and sometimes difficult immigrant experience and the cultural and political upheavals of the contemporary America she lived in, that we will come to know in her books and her life.

3

Silence

She was born Maxine Ting Ting Hong on October 27, 1940, in Stockton, California. Her parents, Tom Hong and Ying Lan Chew Hong, were immigrants from southern China. They both came from the village of Sun Woi, near Canton (today called Guangzhou). Maxine was the oldest child—two children had been born to the Hongs while they lived in China, but neither survived past childhood.

Despite their village background, Maxine's parents were well-educated and literate. Indeed, one of her fondest childhood memories was listening to them recite classic Chinese poetry, as well as the folktales, songs, and rhymes of their village. Her father had, in fact, studied to be a poet, and while he was never able to achieve his dream, the family love of literature paid off with their oldest daughter, as she explained in an interview with Karen Horton:

> The family, most of the people, were not writers. They were readers. They were literate. I think that's very

important in that most people in China were illiterate. My family was special. They could read, and they read poetry . . . so I feel I come from a tradition of literate people, even though they weren't writers.

Her father immigrated to the United States in 1924. In China he had been a scholar and teacher, but he was neither in the United States, largely because of the language barrier. Instead, he was forced to find work doing manual labor, making money however he could and hoping to save enough to bring his family to live with him.

It would take 15 years before he was able to do so. After years of struggle, like many Chinese immigrants before and after him, he opened a laundry with three friends. The business was a success, and Hong was able to live well and send his wife money to join him in the United States.

During their 15-year separation, his wife, Ying Lan (also known as Brave Orchid), had had to experience life in rural China on her own. She had been forced to suffer the deaths of their two children without the support of her husband. She was a strong woman, though, and managed to study medicine and become a doctor.

In some respects, Brave Orchid and her husband were very different people when they finally reunited in New York City. He was well on the way to becoming an American and had grown accustomed to living in his new home. For Brave Orchid, the United States was a whole new world, but one she soon adapted to.

Unfortunately for the Hongs, though, Tom Hong's business partners turned out to be untrustworthy. They teamed up against him and took complete control of the laundry. In response, the Hongs moved from New York City to Stockton, California, where he found work managing an illegal gambling house.

An arched bridge crosses over a canal near a rural Chinese village, in a photograph from 1909. Both of Maxine Hong Kingston's parents were from a small village in southern China. Her father came to the United States in 1924; her mother was not able to join him for 15 years.

His job was to pretend to be the owner of the house on the frequent occasions when the police raided the place and arrested everybody in sight. While it might not have been the most prestigious place to work, it did give Hong inspiration when naming his new daughter, who was born shortly after their move to California. In her book *China Men*, Kingston claims that "my father found a name for me too at the gambling house. 'He named you,' said MaMa, 'after a blond gambler who always won. He gave you her lucky American name.'"

While Maxine's name may have been lucky, it was a difficult time for the Hongs. Tom Hong worked 12 hours a day with no holidays. Maxine's mother worked as well, as a servant to the family of the gambling-house owner: ironing clothes for 12 people and bathing 10 children. It was not the life that Brave Orchid, a trained doctor, imagined herself having in the United States. "We've turned into slaves. . . . I've turned into the servant of a woman who can't read. Maybe we should go back to China," she is quoted as saying in *China Men*.

There were other problems as well. The Hongs, like most people, dreamed of owning their own house. On two occasions, they found a house they could afford. Since neither Tom Hong nor his wife spoke English with any amount of fluency, they relied on Tom's boss to handle the purchasing negotiations. Both times, the boss bought the house himself, claiming it was in the Hongs' best interest; he then rented the house to them. Finally getting wise, on the third occasion, the Hongs handled the transaction themselves and were finally able to own the house they wanted.

It was an exact replica of the owner's house, with the same floor plan, the same gingerbread molding. It was, according to *China Men*, "the biggest most run-down of the houses; it had been a boarding house for old China Men." The house was in a rough neighborhood of Stockton. So rough, in fact, that in *The Woman Warrior*, Kingston tells how her mother "locked her children in the house so we couldn't look at dead slum people." The house was close to railroad tracks, which served as a memorial to the great-grandfather who had helped build America's transcontinental railroad. The Hongs paid $6,000 for the house—$6,000 in hard-earned cash, carefully saved over time and many long hours of hard work.

The family's hard times, though, were not over. During World War II, there was a crackdown on illegal gambling houses in California, and after one police raid too many, Maxine's father was out of work. He entered a period of severe depression, one in which he spent his days sitting at home, staring at the floor. He seemed lost, living without a purpose. The family's savings were being spent, so Maxine's mother went out to work herself, toiling long hours in the fields and canneries of the San Joaquin Valley.

Tom Hong's only interest seemed to be reading the morning paper, *The Gold Mountain News*. Every morning he would be up from his chair and waiting at the front door for it to be delivered. Once it arrived, he would stretch out the reading experience as long as possible: Putting on his gold-rimmed glasses and assembling his smoking equipment, he would read every part of the paper, including the date on each page, the page numbers, even the want ads.

Eventually, though, he pulled himself out of his depression, getting out of his chair to chase his misbehaving children. (By this time, Maxine had five younger brothers and sisters.) Once out of his chair, he did not return, and given the chance to buy a new business from a friend, he jumped at the opportunity. With that, he was back in the laundry business, and the family soon celebrated the grand opening of the New Port Laundry on El Dorado Street.

GROWING UP

Maxine, like the rest of her family, spent many long hours working in the laundry, but like any other young girl, she spent most of her time in school. As with so many other children of immigrants, school was a difficult challenge for Maxine at the beginning.

Kingston's parents, as did most of the Chinese who lived in Stockton at that time, came from the village of Sun Woi. The dialect of Cantonese spoken there, known as "Say Yup," was the language that Maxine grew up hearing, the language she grew up speaking. When she entered school, Maxine spoke virtually no English.

Not only did she have a language barrier, but believe it or not, Kingston says she had had almost no contact with white people before entering public school. She talked about this in a series of lectures and discussions at the University of California, Santa Cruz, in 1989:

> I guess for the first five years of my life I never saw any white people unless they came as a milkman ghost or welfare ghost. And as long as you don't know the true humanity of a person, they're just a ghost. That's a translation of the Chinese.

To young Maxine and her family, white people, in all their "otherness," were like ghosts—strange creatures, not easily understood. But more than that—these "ghosts" were likely to pull them away from their traditional life, from their very "Chinaness," into a new, different life as Americans.

So to help maintain her "Chinaness," Maxine also attended the Chung Wah Chinese School for American Children every day after school from five o'clock until eight o'clock and from nine o'clock on Sundays. There, students were taught how to write and speak Chinese. She attended Chung Wah for seven years but had mixed feelings about the experience, as she said in a lecture at the University of California, Santa Cruz:

> The education is very archaic in that the method is the same as in classical times, which is to memorize. They didn't explain anything. It's just rote memory and

learning many words that you don't hear used. At about the sixth or seventh year they began giving you litera- ture, but in the beginning, almost everything is taught in forms, so everything was a kind of poetic language. Seventh grade is just barely beginning to be able to read real literature. It's just about ready to read the newspa- per and I couldn't go on.

Maxine was fortunate, though, because she was still able to get a knowledge of Chinese classical poetry and literature from her parents. They sang poetry to her. They told her the classic sagas. In fact, even such Western tales as Robinson Crusoe and Doctor Doolittle became Chinese when told by her parents.

Kingston has described her mother as a "champion talker" who taught her children with what she calls "talk stories," sto- ries that included myth, legend, family history, and ghost tales, all blended together to form one narrative that was at once both true and fictional. In Pin-chia Feng's biography, Kingston is quoted as saying, "Night after night my mother would talk- story until we fell asleep. I could not tell where the stories left off and the dreams began."

Brave Orchid used these stories to educate her children and to bring Chinese tradition into their lives. Sometimes, though, the lessons of these traditional tales did not fit into the mod- ern world of American culture and sent decidedly mixed sig- nals. While she would tell her daughter of the legendary brave woman warrior, Fa Mu Lan, at other times she would warn her daughter that her role as a woman was to grow up to be a wife and slave. It would take years for Kingston to reconcile those two lessons and to reinterpret traditional Chinese tales with a feminist slant.

EXPRESSING HERSELF

Although Maxine grew up speaking Chinese, English proved more difficult. When she entered school, she did not speak a word of English; shy and afraid, she withdrew into silence. As she said in *The Woman Warrior*, "When I went to kindergarten and had to speak English for the first time, I became silent."

Her teachers in public school did not know what to do with her. For that first year, Maxine spoke to no one at school and would not even ask permission to use the bathroom. It is hard to believe, given the masterful writer that she later became, but Maxine actually flunked kindergarten, was often sent to sit in the corner, and even scored zero on an IQ test when she colored the examination page black. Interestingly, when Maxine's younger sister entered school, she was silent for *three* years. Other Chinese girls did not talk in class either. It is probable that insecurity about language, in addition to the lesser role Chinese women generally had within the family, caused the girls to retreat behind a wall of silence. (It was different at the Chinese language school. There, as Kingston says, "the girls were not mute." They chanted along with the boys during periods of reciting and screamed and yelled on the playground during recess.)

Unwilling to speak in her public-school classes, Maxine turned to painting as her means of communication. By and large, for the period of Maxine's silence, her paintings generally were images in black, as she recounted in *The Woman Warrior*, "I painted layers of black over houses and flowers and suns, and when I drew on the blackboard, I put a layer of chalk on top. I was making a stage curtain, and it was the moment before the curtain parted or rose."

Not surprisingly, Maxine's teachers became alarmed at her massive output of black paintings and called her parents in to discuss the matter. Her teacher showed them all of their daughter's works, "curling and crackling, all alike and black."

Unfortunately, Maxine's parents, despite their years in the United States, did not understand English well and were unable to comprehend exactly what the teacher was trying to tell them about the meaning of all that black. Maxine's black period, though, was coming to an end. She was beginning to find new ways to communicate, ways that would allow her to "speak" to the world.

STORYTELLING

In a 1989 interview with Paul Skenazy, Kingston said:

> As far back as I can remember I was a storyteller, and before I could write, I was inventing stories. I don't know whether I was born that way or whether it was the way I was raised. But I was raised in a storytelling culture, and one of my first memories, which I wrote about in *China Men*, is of the sound of horses outside. My uncles had vegetable wagons that were pulled by horses. They were old renovated stagecoaches, and I loved the rhythm of the hooves. My mother took me to the window, and she and I invented a song to sing to the uncles. She called it teasing. She'd say, "We're going to tease them," and then we'd sing the song for them. So she always raised me with, "Let's invent a song."

Maxine began to write when she was around eight years old. Kingston insists that she is a "born writer," meaning that she is someone who simply *has* to write—it is as important and basic and essential to her as eating and breathing are. As she said in an interview with Kay Bonetti in 1986, "I feel like I'm a born writer—then when you're celebrating, you put it into words, and when you're mourning, you put it into words. There's this desire always to find the words for life and for the invisible and for the visible and for the imagination."

There was no question, though, in which language she would be writing—it would have to be English. The reason? The dialect of Chinese that she and her parents speak, Say Yup, has no written form. The question then becomes, how to present the sounds, slang, and dialogue of Say Yup in English? Oddly enough, it turned out that using English was the best way for her to present the Chinese experience on paper, as she explained in a 1993 interview with Neila C. Seshachari:

> I think that I first contended with these questions [about language] when I was about seven years old, and, you know, my first language is Chinese, and I only knew people who spoke Chinese. I talked story and I invented poems and made up songs and I heard stories, but when I began to know the English language and somewhere around eight years old, I started to write, and the English language was so . . . bright, full of freedom, because the English language is so easy, and I thought . . . I can write Chinese in English. . . . You speak Chinese and then the written language is completely different. There's no system. It's one word at a time. But all of a sudden, with the 26 letters in the English language you can write anything, so I just felt I had the most powerful tool, and I felt free to express myself.

With that understanding, that breakthrough, the need to express herself through language became an overwhelming feeling. The first work that she clearly remembers writing was a poem, and it was a transformative experience, as she told Gary Kubota:

> I started writing when I was nine and I remember the incident quite clearly. I was sitting in a class, and all of

a sudden this poem came to me. I wrote 25 verses in something like a trance. I don't recall what the class was about. Later, I wrote prose.

She described the process further in her book *Hawai'i One Summer*:

And yet it was in Mrs. Garner's classroom that I discovered that I could write poems. I remember the very moment the room filled with a light that would have been white except that the warm light off the wooden desks (with the inkwell holes and the pencil grooves) suffused it with yellow—and out of the air and into my head and down my arm and out my fingers came ten, twenty verses in an a-b-b-a rhyme. The poem was about flying; I flew . . . I wrote down the music and the voices I heard.

Maxine quickly developed the habit of writing down her thoughts and ideas, even going as far as to clear space in her parents' crowded storeroom for her papers and notes. As she told Paul Skenazy, "I thought it was the most richness when my parents had a pantry and I rearranged all the cans and preserves and everything so that I'd have a shelf of my own. I put my books and papers there, and then I cleared out a space and I put a table in there and a chair and I locked the door. That was the most space that I had for a long time."

While writing poetry and other forms of creative writing came relatively easily to her, writing prose in a way that satisfied her teachers was more of a challenge. She described the difficulties she faced in a 1977 interview with Gary Kubota:

When I was in high school, I didn't know about different forms of writing. I always wrote in my story form

A woman at a newsstand in Nanjing, China, reads a newspaper article about a change in leadership in the country's government in 2002. To be able to read a newspaper in the Chinese language, a person needs to know about 3,000 characters. Most educated Chinese people know 6,000 to 7,000 characters.

THE CHINESE LANGUAGE

Unlike the English language, which is made up of just 26 letters that are combined to make words, the Chinese language is a bit more complicated. Written Chinese centers on characters known as *hanzi*, which are written as though within imaginary rectangular blocks, arranged in vertical columns, read from top to bottom down a column, and right to left across columns. (A more informal form of written Chinese has emerged online in chat rooms, but it is almost never seen outside of that format.)

These Chinese characters have evolved over time from early forms of hieroglyphs, or pictorial symbols. While most people believe that all Chinese characters are either pictographs (a picture that represents a word or an idea) or ideographs (a graphic character that indicates the meaning of a thing without indicating the sounds used to say it), in truth, most characters are combinations of pictographs or ideographs *and* the phonetic components used to sound out the word.

Sound complicated? It is. Even though the People's Republic of China introduced the Simplified Chinese character system in 1954 to promote literacy, a well-educated Chinese person today recognizes 6,000 to 7,000 characters—some 3,000 characters are required just to read a newspaper. Remarkably, a large unabridged dictionary, such as the Kangxi Dictionary, contains more than 40,000 characters, although less than a quarter of those characters are in common use today.

and got away with it. I never understood what teachers meant when they assigned us term papers. Once our class was assigned to write about produces of California. I wrote a story about those hoboes who were hitch-hiking around California and who visited cities and towns that specialized in different produce. I was more interested in the hoboes than the products.

Soon enough, though, she began to get the hang of writing essays. Indeed, she became so good at it that, when she was just 15 years old, her essay "I Am an American" was published in *American Girl*, the magazine of the Girl Scouts of America. Not only was her essay published, but she won a $5 prize as well.

In the essay, we can see some of the ideas and themes that Kingston has used throughout her career—namely, asserting the value of being Chinese, as well as using the idea that one can be Chinese and a "good American" at the same time. She discussed the essay in a 2007 interview on National Public Radio:

> I worked out the idea that you don't have to be white to be an American. But all the time I was aware that both my parents were illegals and I had to be very careful to write in such a way that I can insist on our being American without giving away their illegal status. . . .
>
> I wanted to assert myself as an American . . . and it was also in reaction to the prejudice and racism that was all around me. And the only way I could defend myself was to positively set out the really good American values.

Despite her success in the classic essay form, it still felt confining to Maxine. The way she wanted to write, the stories she wanted to tell, the voices she wanted to get on paper did not fit easily into standardized forms. Her writing was at its best, she felt, when her teachers said, "Write whatever you want." With those words, she had the freedom to write as herself.

SEEING YOURSELF IN BOOKS

Of course, like most budding writers, Maxine loved to read. There was one problem, though: There were no characters like her in any of the popular books for young adults of the day.

Between the Generations

"YOU TRIED TO CUT OFF MY TONGUE"

In the section "A Song for a Barbarian Reed Pipe" in *The Woman Warrior*, Maxine Hong Kingston tells about a tirade she had against her parents one day while they were working at the family laundry:

The only reason I flunked kindergarten was because you couldn't teach me English, and you gave me a zero IQ. I've brought my IQ up, though. They say I'm smart now. Things follow in lines at school. They take stories and teach us to turn them into essays. I don't need anybody to pronounce English words for me. I can figure them out myself. I'm going to get scholarships, and I'm going away. And at college I'll have the people I like for friends. I don't care if their great-great-grandfather died of TB. I don't care if they were our enemies in China four thousand years ago. . . . I'm going to college. And I'm not going to Chinese school anymore. I'm going to run for office at American school, and I'm going to join clubs. I'm going to get enough offices and clubs on my record to get into college. And I can't stand Chinese school anyway: the kids are rowdy and mean, fighting all night. And I don't want to listen to any more of your stories: they have no logic. They scramble me up. You lie with stories. You won't tell me a story and then say, 'This is a true story,' or, 'This is just a story.' I can't tell the difference. I don't even know what your real names are. I can't tell what's real and what you make up. Ha! You can't stop me from talking. You tried to cut off my tongue, but it didn't work.

People of Chinese origin, like most non-white people, simply did not exist in the literature of the day. On the rare occasions when they did appear, it was generally in an unattractive, stereotypical way. Even classic novels, like Louisa May Alcott's

Little Women, proved to be a difficult reading experience for Kingston, as she told interviewer Jody Hoy:

> In Louisa May Alcott one of her characters marries a . . .
> I guess she calls him a Chinaman, with a long pigtail.
> He was so funny, he was so weird and different. I was
> reading along, identifying with the March sisters, when
> I came across this funny-looking Chinaman. It popped
> out of the book. I'd been pushed into my place. I was
> him, I wasn't those March girls.

Imagine not having any books to read with characters like yourself. Imagine if the only characters in books who were even remotely like you were there as figures to be laughed at. For Maxine, the experience was painful enough that it, as she put it, ejected her out of literature for a time. Fortunately for Maxine, she soon discovered a book that showed her there were other possibilities.

The book was *Fifth Chinese Daughter* by Jade Snow Wong, and it brought her back in. The book, which tells the story of Wong's San Francisco childhood, changed everything for Maxine. For the first time, despite all of the books she had read, the main character was somebody like her. The book opened her eyes to what could be written about in literature, and, perhaps most importantly, it showed her what *she* could write about, as she explained to Jody Hoy:

> For the first time I saw a Chinese-American charac-
> ter, and it was told from the point of view of a young
> girl. For the first time I could see a person somewhat
> like myself in literature. I had been trying to write
> about people who were blond, or a beautiful redhead
> on her horse, because those were the people who were
> in the books.

Maxine Hong Kingston said that, as a child, she never saw herself represented in books until she read *Fifth Chinese Daughter* by Jade Snow Wong *(above)*. The book, published in 1950, told the story of Wong's childhood in San Francisco.

She elaborated on this in a 1989 interview with William Satake Blauvelt:

> There were such wonderful illustrations of little kids that looked like me, and most importantly, written by a Chinese-American woman. So, she gave me this great welcome and send-off, so I continued writing.

All of which is not to say, of course, that Maxine's life revolved entirely around books, writing, and her family. Like any high school student, she had friends, the normal insecurities about fitting in, and the everyday problems associated with adolescence and growing up. Even so, by the time she graduated from Edison High School in 1958, the one-time kindergartner with a zero IQ now had a straight "A" average and a journalism scholarship to the University of California, Berkeley, the college she had wanted to attend since she was a child. For the first time in her life, she would be leaving home, and she hoped to achieve some level of independence from her family and culture.

But would she? Like many Chinese-American parents, the Hongs wanted to make certain that their daughter would not have to support herself doing the kind of physical labor that they had done in the United States. Instead, they wanted her to be a professional: a doctor, perhaps, or a mathematician or an engineer, an occupation that would give her and her family prestige and security. Bowing to family pressure, when 17-year-old Maxine Hong entered Berkeley, she was not an English major. She would study engineering in an attempt to do herself and her family proud.

4

Berkeley
to Hawaii

For the first time in her life, Maxine Hong was living away from her home and family. At first it was difficult, living without the family and community structure that had been her security blanket her entire life. While she quickly made friends and created her own community at college, she soon found herself questioning her course of study. She had wanted to be an engineering major because it seemed the practical choice—the best way for her to ensure that she would be able to make a living and the best way to honor and please her family. Her dream to become a writer, however, refused to die.

Hong did not remain an engineering student for long. Although she was certainly smart enough to complete the work, her heart just was not in it. As a "born writer," she would never be happy doing engineering work or any other work, for that matter, that did not involve writing. She would have to get up the courage to defy her parents, strike her own path, study what she wanted, and become the writer she knew she was meant to be.

She started slowly, working on the university's student newspaper, *The Californian*. But that was not enough. She was miserable studying engineering—there was no way to avoid making the break. Hong switched majors, leaving the engineering department and entering the English department. It was a liberating experience, she told interviewer Marilyn Chin:

> I always thought taking English was just fun. There was no good reason for doing it. When I went from engineering to English, I felt I had abdicated all my responsibilities! I was just living life for the fun of it. I guess it was the way I was raised, but everything had to be hard. Engineering was worth it because it was hard. But English was easy for me, so I shouldn't do anything that was easy. I thought it was like that. There was something wrong with me if I did something that was easy and fun.

Of course, studying English was not *always* fun and easy. Sometimes Hong found herself wondering if she had made the right decision. Most of her classes were in critical theory, classes that led her to question if she even had the talent to become a writer, as she recalled to interviewer Paul Skenazy:

> I was going to read and talk about books. But the education was in critical theory, and what was happening to me as a writer was that no sooner would I create something than I would criticize and destroy it. I kept thinking maybe I should be in a writing program. I think my standards were too high. But I used to go to the tennis courts in Berkeley. I just saw how faithful the tennis pros were. They just kept practicing and practicing, and they didn't take breaks all the time. I'd

In the American Grain, by poet William Carlos Williams (1883–1963), had a tremendous influence on Maxine Hong Kingston. In the book, Williams uses myths to tell the history of America. Kingston would use myth and history to uncover truths, as well.

have my typewriter there, and I thought, "I'm going to be just like them." And then I began.

Not only did Hong regain confidence in herself as a writer, she was also introduced through her literature classes to two books that would have a profound influence on her as a person and as a writer: *In the American Grain* by the American poet William Carlos Williams and *Orlando* by the British novelist Virginia Woolf.

In the first book, *In the American Grain*, Williams tells the story of America by narrating its myths. The history he tells is not completely accurate, but it has the truth that comes with myth. As Kingston described it to interviewer Kay Bonetti, "He starts with the Vikings and he ends at the Civil War with Abraham Lincoln as a woman who is walking through the fields with his/her shawl and looking at the fallen soldiers, and I thought that was the truest book of American history I had ever read. . . . That is the way I want to think about American history, about history, in the mythic, true way." As we shall see, that is what Kingston does in her own books, combining history and myth to tell a story that is, on a poetic level, truer than using either history or myth on its own.

While William Carlos Williams showed Hong the possibilities of using myth and history to get at certain truths, Virginia Woolf helped to liberate her as a writer. In Woolf's groundbreaking novel *Orlando*, published in 1928, the title character begins life as a man in Elizabethan England, wakes up as a woman with the same personality and intellect halfway through the book, and lives to be more than 400 without visibly aging. "Reading Virginia Woolf's *Orlando* was an event," she told Jody Hoy. "It's all right to make your man turn into a woman; it's all right to have a century of time flow by here and a moment of time flow by there. She showed me various freedoms I could take in writing."

(Not only did these works inspire Kingston as a young writer, they still do to this day. "When I read Virginia Woolf's *Orlando* or William Carlos Williams's *In the American Grain*, I can feel like I'm dying, or I'm stuck, both in life and in work. I read those books and then I start flowing again," she told Marilyn Chin.)

GRADUATION, MARRIAGE, AND FAMILY

Maxine Hong graduated in 1962 from the University of California, Berkeley, with a B.A. in English. A number of years would pass, however, before she put her degree to good use. Just months after graduation, Hong married her college sweetheart, an aspiring actor named Earll Kingston. Less than two years later, the couple's only child, Joseph Lawrence Chung Mei Kingston, was born. Now just 23 years old, Kingston was a wife and a mother and undecided about where her life and career should go.

Curiously, even though she had received her degree in English, she still felt in some ways that she was a painter, not a writer. She explained the reasons behind this in a 1986 interview with Kay Bonetti:

> After college I thought that I was a painter because I always see pictures, and I see visions before the words come, and it's always a secondary step to find the words. So at one time I thought that I could go directly from picture to picture because when I write I want the readers to see the pictures. So why not forget the words and just paint pictures?

Kingston painted for a year after graduation before she came to a startling realization. She recognized that she had already put in 20 years of hard work learning how to use words. To become as good a painter as she *knew* she was a writer, she would have to paint for another 20 years. With that, she put the paints away (except for her own enjoyment) and began to concentrate on writing.

Another book that had a great impact on Maxine Hong Kingston as a young writer was *Orlando* by Virginia Woolf (1882–1941). *Orlando* showed Kingston the many liberties she could take as a writer.

She was not in a position, however, in which she could settle into the role of a starving, struggling writer; not with a young family to help support. So Kingston went back to school, taking classes to receive her teaching certificate at the University of California, Berkeley. After working as a student teacher at Oakland Technical High School, Kingston taught English and mathematics from 1965 to 1967 at Oakland Technical High School and at Sunset High School in Hayward, California.

For someone who grew up silent, who hated the sounds that came out of her throat, and still referred to them as her "duck voice," teaching, which means speaking to a class of students for hours at a time, proved to be a personal and physical challenge. Yet, it turned out to be an important part of her life, one that she has maintained off and on for more than 40 years. As she said in a 1986 interview with Jody Hoy:

> I taught high school mostly. That is the hardest job on earth. If you can be a teacher and last for a few years, you can do anything. That's what did it. When I began teaching, I still had my duck voice, and by the time I was through, I could do anything. . . . Perhaps that was my way of working out of the voice. A teacher can speak to everyone, a teacher can control mobs. You can break up fights, you can teach a rock to read.

Kingston was teaching, being a wife and mother, and participating in the protests against the Vietnam War—the years 1965 to 1967 were busy and important ones for her and her husband. But, by 1967, both she and Earll had had enough of San Francisco and Berkeley, enough of the war protests, enough of the spiraling-out-of-control drug scene. The couple packed up their belongings and their three-year-old son and fled to Hawaii, where they hoped to find an island paradise they could use as an escape from the war. They found the island paradise, but it proved to bring the war closer to them than it had ever been. As Kingston told Gary Kubota, "Hawaii had its own problems, and with the presence of the military here, the Vietnam War was even more real on these islands."

American troops came through Hawaii on their way to their tours of duty in Vietnam; on-duty soldiers came to Hawaii for their periods of R&R (Rest and Relaxation). In no time, Kingston and her husband were more involved in the antiwar movement than ever before. The couple helped to counsel veterans and even worked in a church sanctuary for soldiers who had gone AWOL (Absent Without Leave).

AVOIDING THE VIETNAM WAR

While living in Hawaii, Maxine Hong Kingston spent time counseling American soldiers who had gone AWOL (Absent Without Leave). There were far more Americans who did whatever they could to avoid fighting in the Vietnam War to begin with, including leaving the United States entirely. These men became known as draft dodgers.

For the middle and the upper classes, there were numerous ways to avoid fighting in Vietnam. (For the poor, it was another matter altogether, which resulted in the saying, "Rich man's war, poor man's fight.") Serving in the U.S. Navy (as Kingston's brother did), Air Force, or Coast Guard were options. Divinity students were exempt from the draft, so large numbers of men found an unexpected calling to enter the ministry or rabbinate. Medical or psychological deferments were another possibility. In essence, there were enough loopholes in the draft law that, for those with the means, it was possible to avoid being sent to Vietnam.

Those without means or influence had to resort to other ways to avoid fighting in the war. Rather than submit to

Kingston listened to their stories of the war and observed them enjoying their R&R. "I saw three soldiers, one crippled and two bandaged, jumping in the waves with their clothes on, splashing one another, cavorting. Glad to be alive, I thought, glad to be out of Vietnam alive," she wrote in *Hawai'i One Summer*.

The couple, strong in their belief that the war was wrong, withdrew from the mainstream of society as much as possible, certain that, by doing so, they were, at the very least, not providing any assistance or support for the war or the government that supported the war. Initially, they refused to get new jobs, feeling that it was their duty as pacifists *not* to work in a war

conscription, tens of thousands of young men migrated to Canada, which did not support the war in Vietnam. All told, nearly 100,000 draft dodgers left the country, an estimated 50,000 to 90,000 of whom went to Canada; others remained in hiding in the United States. Draft evasion was not a criminal offense under Canadian law; and even though deserting the military was an offense, Canadian officials instructed border guards not to ask questions related to the issue. Canada became, in effect, a "safe haven" for those who refused to fight in the Vietnam War.

The draft ended in 1973 as did American involvement in the war. But those who traveled abroad faced imprisonment or forced military service if they returned home, and the United States continued to prosecute draft dodgers after the end of the Vietnam War. Finally, in 1977, President Jimmy Carter issued an amnesty in the form of a pardon to all remaining draft evaders, as part of a goal to unite the country after a long and bitterly divisive war. Many returned home, but according to sociologist John Hagan, nearly 50,000 remained in Canada.

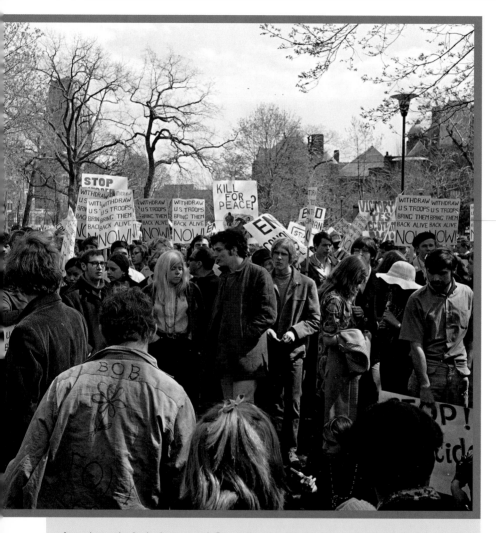

American draft dodgers and Canadian students demonstrated in May 1968 in Toronto, Canada, against the sale of arms to the United States. To avoid the U.S. draft, 50,000 to 90,000 young men fled to Canada during the Vietnam War.

economy. (A pacifist is someone who is opposed to war on principle and to ever using violence to settle disputes.)

The Kingstons found a small apartment for just $90 a month on top of a grocery store on the Hawaiian island of Oahu. They found a bunk bed in an abandoned house and "borrowed" a park bench to use as a sofa. They learned that "a human being could live out of the Dumpsters behind the supermarkets. Blocks of cheese had only a little extra mold on them. Tear off the outer leaves, and the cabbage heads were perfectly fresh," Kingston wrote in *Hawai'i One Summer.*

While this lifestyle may have seemed to the Kingstons an honorable way to maintain their distance from the war, with a young son to care for, it soon proved impractical. Bowing to reality, Maxine returned to work as a teacher. For the next 10 years, she taught at a variety of schools in Hawaii, including Kahuku High School and the Kahaluu Drop-in School. She also taught English as a second language at Honolulu Business College and language arts at Kailua High School.

For an activist who longed to make a difference in the world, who strove to improve society, the work was greatly rewarding. Kingston relished exposing students to the possibilities of literature, and loved encouraging them to write and learn about themselves through their writing.

Remembering what it was like when she felt that her teachers' assignments had stifled her creativity, Kingston worked hard to *encourage* her students' creativity. She explained her teaching techniques in a lecture at the University of California, Santa Cruz:

> I want the students to be free to write about what they want. I then come at them with form and don't even touch the content. That's something that's theirs, that's personal. I tell them, for example, that all I want is a hundred pages of anything by the end of the semester. I did not grade on content or even style, but just quantity. I thought maybe that after they got bored with pages and pages of telling me what they ate every day,

and what classes they took, they would go more into their feelings and personal lives. The way I graded was a hundred pages was an A, 80 was a B, 60 was a C, 40 was a D, and 20 was an F. Actually I've had some wonderful, true writing, because some of them would be uninhibited and try to get through this as fast as possible, so just by going fast and putting down as much as they could, they were breaking through some kind of block.

At times, though, Kingston worried that by using this method, her students would enter college without knowing how to give their writing shape and form. So on occasion, she would pull back from unstructured writing and use exercises to show them how to give structure to their work.

Teaching in Hawaii posed its own set of special challenges. Many of Kingston's students were of Asian descent. Like Kingston herself when she was growing up, they saw themselves as outsiders and as inferior to the majority non-Asian population. She worked hard to help her students overcome these feelings, as she explained to Paul Skenazy:

A lot of my students were Japanese American, and a lot of what they enjoyed writing was love stories. Their love stories were always about blonde people, white people. These are the looks that are worthy of love, as they see it. This is all they see, so I would spend a lot of time correcting that. Mostly it was just a matter of asking them, well, what if this was a love story that had a person in it who looked like you? Can you just change it and see what happens? . . . I think this taught them to see the beauty of their own looks, and to break out of the stereotypes.

DOING HER OWN WORK

Despite her busy schedule of teaching, antiwar work, and parenting, Kingston still found time to write. Her work began to be published: The article "Literature for a Scientific Age: Lorenz' *King Solomon's Ring*" appeared in the January 1973 issue of *English Journal*, and *Your Reading: A Booklist for Junior High Students* was published by the National Council of Teachers of English. These works, carefully written and organized, helped to reassure Kingston that she could still write in a coherent manner that others could easily understand. Although the work was gratifying, it still wasn't *hers*. That, though, would soon be changing.

Several factors played a role in giving Kingston the ability to sit down and write the book she had always dreamed of writing. As American involvement in the Vietnam War ended in 1973 with the withdrawal of U.S. troops, so too did the antiwar movement. This gave Kingston the time, the freedom, and the emotional liberation necessary to concentrate more on her own work. Her son, Joseph Lawrence, was growing up, which also allowed her more time and space for her work.

And, in its own way, Hawaii played a role as well. In a 1979 interview with Karen Horton, Kingston explained that:

> Hawaii is a wonderful place to work. It is conducive to creativity. The visual things, the sensory impressions are strong in Hawaii. And you need that to make you aware of the sensory experiences that go into the writing. That doesn't mean that I write what I see around me. The sense of being more alive is very important to creating. The quiet in Hawaii, well, that makes me able to think. It keeps your intuitions open and that's important.

It was now time to write the book she had been thinking about and planning since she was a young girl. It would bring together history, myth, and family history to tell her own story. The book would take two years to write and would make her name on the literary landscape and open doors for Asian-American writers throughout the United States.

5

A Girlhood Among Ghosts

"You must not tell anyone," my mother said, "what I am about to tell you."

—opening sentence, *The Woman Warrior*

The book was *The Woman Warrior: Memoirs of a Girlhood Among Ghosts*. Although most of it was written while she was in Hawaii, Kingston has admitted that she had been working on the book since she was a child. "A kid doesn't yet have the vocabulary, although I had the feelings. I had a lot of feelings, and a lot of stories. In some sense you could say that I was working on these books [*The Woman Warrior* and the subsequent volume *China Men*] for 20 or 30 years, but in another sense I wrote them just a few years ago," she said in a 1980 interview with Arturo Islas.

So, how exactly did she go about writing her first book? Kingston has said that she has two primary ways of getting the words on the page. The first, which dates back to her very first poem, is when the writing comes to her suddenly, and she feels an overwhelming need to write and create. "I don't have a controlled method of going about that. I might be anywhere when it comes, and I could end up writing all over the floor or up the walls and not know what is going on. It's like having a fit," she told interviewer Timothy Pfaff.

She went on to explain to him that the second way is more conscious, but ideally leads to the same ecstatic state of trance and creativity. It involves "following a trail made by words themselves—by sitting down and writing, writing crazy, writing anything, fast. The words induce the vision. That rush, that outpouring—that vision or high or whatever it is—doesn't last very long. A lot of writing gets done in a very short time, but it's not very good writing.... It has to be reworked. Most of my time goes into that rewriting, which I have much control over."

(This second style, which basically involved just writing, writing, writing, sounds suspiciously similar to the way of writing she encouraged in her high school students. Write as much as you can, as fast as you can, and something good will emerge from it.)

What Kingston was looking for was a way to achieve what William Carlos Williams accomplished in his book *In the American Grain*—a way to blend the real with the unreal, the fictitious, and the mythic. Throughout *The Woman Warrior*, there is always an underlying tension as to what is real and what is not, what is true and what seems to be true. For example, in the section entitled "At the Western Palace," Kingston tells in detail the tale of her mother's sister, Moon Orchid, and her encounter with the husband from whom she had been separated for 30 years.

At the beginning of the next section, entitled "A Song for a Barbarian Reed Pipe," Kingston admits that she did not witness the events in the story about Moon Orchid. She had heard a partial version of the story from her brother; thus, the story is a blend of the real and the imagined. Using her skills as a story-teller, Kingston tells a story that should be true, or, that *is* true in the sense that it *feels* true.

According to Deborah L. Madsen in her study of Kingston, this style, which Kingston herself calls "convoluted," is something she consciously strives to achieve. The reason? To Kingston, life itself does not always conform to a simple structured narrative with a neatly defined beginning, middle, and end. Instead, she feels that life is more complicated than that: Life itself is confused and convoluted, with no easily defined beginnings or ends, and writing that attempts to show truth should reflect that confusion.

Part of the basis of Kingston's desire for ambiguity, or uncertainty, in her work is that the origin of many of the stories that Kingston tells are not from written narrative but from oral storytelling, the tales and myths told to her by her mother when she was a girl. When a story is put down on paper, it is made permanent and unchanging. But when a tale is told orally, it constantly changes with each telling. Which then, Kingston continually asks the careful reader, is the true or real version?

In Kingston's work, even the myths change. As a writer, her interest does not lie in what the myths were in China. What interests her is what the myths became upon their retelling here in America. "We have to do more than record myth," she told interviewer Timothy Pfaff. "The way I keep the old Chinese myths alive is by telling them in a new American way."

In addition to the continuous mingling of myth and reality, non-Asian readers may be surprised to discover the constant image of ghosts working their way through *The Woman Warrior*. As Madsen points out, in the world of the book, "ghosts are those who threaten Chinese traditions by drawing people away from Chinese culture or by subverting it. . . . These threats to traditional culture are rendered void and deprived of reality when they are thought of as ghosts. Most terrifying to the young Kingston were the ghosts of the dead and tortured Chinese people that her mother conjured up in her stories."

By blending history and myth, the stories of her family with those of Chinese legend, the real world and that of ghosts and unreality, Kingston was able to create a new kind of work. In it, Kingston compares the stories of her ancestors and of herself with traditional Chinese legend and parables, which helps to explain the meaning of both.

THE WOMAN WARRIOR

As Madsen describes the book in her study of Kingston, *The Woman Warrior* is a narrative that is divided into five linked stories: "No Name Woman," "White Tigers," "Shaman," At the Western Palace," and "A Song for a Barbarian Reed Pipe." Each story focuses on a female character who serves as a representative of the book's narrator. The stories are linked by the unmistakable narrative voice of Kingston, who recalls events from her childhood and the tales that her mother, Brave Orchid, told her. Although the book's structure and narrative style may sound difficult, Kingston's skill as an author and the beauty of her prose help guide the reader to an understanding of her work.

The first story, "No Name Woman," opens with Brave Orchid's warning to her teenage daughter Maxine to keep secret the story she is about to tell. In it, Maxine learns about her father's sister, an aunt she had never known about because of the circumstances surrounding her death.

The story takes place sometime after Brave Orchid's husband, along with his father, brothers, and the husband of his sister, had come to the United States in search of work. Years later, Brave Orchid learns that her sister-in-law had become pregnant, obviously by a man not her husband. The other villagers learn that she is pregnant as well, and on the night before she is to give birth, they raid her house, kill all of her livestock, and destroy the harvest. The next morning, when Brave Orchid goes to the well to fetch the day's water, she discovers that her sister-in-law had drowned herself, along with her newborn child. Shockingly, the sister-in-law's punishment for the sin of having a child with someone other than her husband continues even after her death: To her family, it is as if she had never even existed, which is why she is called "No Name Woman."

It is only at the end of the tale that Kingston learns why her mother has finally chosen to tell her this story. It is to warn Maxine that the same thing could happen to her. "Now that you have started to menstruate, what happened to her could happen to you. Don't humiliate us. You wouldn't like to be forgotten as if you had never been born. The villagers are watchful." Kingston goes on to write, "Those of us in the first American generations have had to figure out how the invisible world the emigrants built around our childhoods fit in solid America." In other words, how do the rules and ghosts and tales of the world of China fit into the world of contemporary America?

In the rest of this section, Kingston talks about her life in Stockton, and perhaps most importantly, both questions and changes the meaning of the narrative her mother had told her. What had actually happened? Had her defenseless aunt been raped? Or had she, separated from her husband for years, fallen in love with another man? What role did Brave Orchid play in her aunt's punishment and death—did she also participate in the raid? Did her aunt drown herself in the well as an act of sorrow and guilt? Or, was it an act of revenge, to poison and curse the village's only water supply? The answers to these questions are left unclear, leaving readers to determine for themselves what they see as the truth.

In part, *The Woman Warrior* was written expressly to tell "No Name Woman's" story—to restore her to her family's history and to revive her memory. Kingston explained to Paul Skenazy, "It's a most terrible kind of murder—to take her out

Xiao Xiangyu, a well-known performer in traditional Yuju Opera, is shown portraying the character of Fa Mu Lan. Maxine Hong Kingston retold the myth of Fa Mu Lan in the "White Tigers" section of *The Woman Warrior*, modernizing the tale to give it new meaning in America.

of memory. I now realize that what I did by writing down her story and giving it my concern and care and finding the words for it, is I have saved her. I realize now that this is the power of art. I gave her a life, I gave her history, I gave her immortality, I gave her meaning."

The next story, "White Tigers," introduces the main symbolic figure of the book—the warrior woman. In this tale, Kingston learns that there are possibilities open to her as a woman that she had not considered, and another ambiguity is displayed. "She [Brave Orchid] said I would grow up as a wife and a slave, but she taught me the song of the warrior woman, Fa Mu Lan. I would have to grow up a warrior woman." (Walt Disney Pictures made an animated film in 1998 telling the same story in a different way. The film is called *Mulan*.)

In Kingston's telling, she herself becomes the warrior Fa Mu Lan, and with her, we relive her years of physical and mental training, her military career, and the very act of disguising herself as a man so that she could lead troops into battle. As part of her training, she spends time alone living in the mountain home of the white tigers, where she experiences mystical visions and learns how to kill from the mysterious white tigers.

When she has completed her training and is a warrior, she returns home in time to take her father's place in the army. Before she leaves for war, her parents carve into her back a full list of all of the injustices and wrongs done to her village that need to be avenged, as Kingston wrote in *The Woman Warrior*:

> My mother caught the blood and wiped the cuts with a cold towel soaked in wine. It hurt terribly—the cuts sharp; the air burning; the alcohol cold, then hot—pain so various. . . . If not for the fifteen years of training, I would have writhed on the floor; I would have had to be held down.

The warrior goes on to lead an army of peasants who re-store justice to the land; she then returns home with honor to her parents and village. The lesson for Kingston? Whatever she does in her life cannot compare to the achievements of Fa Mu Lan. Should her family ever return to China (which she fears they will), she is convinced that, since she is worthless, her par-ents will sell her into slavery. Finally, though, Kingston real-izes the similarities between herself and the woman warrior. Both are seeking revenge for wrongs done to them and their community. Fa Mu Lan will achieve her revenge in physical battle; Kingston will do so by writing about injustice: "The re-porting is the vengeance—not the beheading, not the gutting, but the words."

"White Tigers" is also an excellent example of Kingston's method of modernizing traditional myth to give it a new mean-ing in America, as she explained to Kay Bonetti:

> When the woman warrior has the words carved on her back, that's actually a man's story. It's about a man named Yüch Fei who had the vow carved on his back by his mother. . . . I gave a man's myth to a woman, be-cause it's part of the feminist war that's going on in *The Woman Warrior*, to take the men's stories away from them and give the strength of that story to a woman. . . . It's part of my own freedom to play with the myth, and I do feel that the myths have to be changed and played with all the time, or they die.

The book's third section, "Shaman," tells the story of Brave Orchid's life in China while she waited for her husband to earn enough money to bring her to America. In the story, Brave Or-chid uses the little bit of money that her husband sends her to go to medical school to become a doctor and obstetrician. In a nice juxtaposition, while Brave Orchid is at school learning facts and science, she also has an encounter with a ghost that has been haunting one of the dormitory rooms. Brave Orchid defeats the ghost, proving her own strength and courage, and after graduating, she returns to her village in triumph, in a manner similar to that of the woman warrior. "She had gone away ordinary and come back miraculous, like the ancient magicians who came down from the mountains."

(Interestingly, years after Kingston wrote *The Woman Warrior*, she was talking to her mother and asked her if her battle with the ghost had really happened. "Of course," she replied. "And not only that, but the ghost had a foot sticking out." Kingston thought, "My God, she's still adding [to the story]. I had written it all down that there was this hairy thing, but I didn't write down that it had a foot." Of course, this goes to prove Kingston's point that stories in the oral tradition are in a constant state of change.)

By telling her daughter this story of China, Brave Orchid also left her with terrifying images of sick and dying babies, ghosts, and monsters, which led Kingston to divide her world into that of a normal American girl and that of the nightmarish ghost world of her mother's China. As for Brave Orchid, her life (as well as her daughter's) in America is haunted by a new kind of ghost, just as frightening as the "real" ghosts in China. "Taxi Ghosts, Bus Ghosts, Police Ghosts, Fire Ghosts, Meter Reader Ghosts, Tree Trimming Ghosts, Five-and-Dime Ghosts." But just as Brave Orchid, with bravery and courage, conquered both the Chinese ghosts and the American "ghosts," Kingston herself would have to learn to be brave and courageous.

Brave Orchid has the strength to survive in China and in America, but as we learn in the book's next story, "At the Western Palace," her sister Moon Orchid was not as lucky. Feminine and fragile, she lacks the courage and strength to survive in the United States. She had lived for years alone in China; her husband had come to America, where he not only found success as a doctor but a new wife and family as well. After years of goading from Brave Orchid, Moon Orchid came to America to reclaim her husband, but after being rejected by

PEARL S. BUCK

Before the publication of Maxine Hong Kingston's *The Woman Warrior*, the best known literary depictions of Chinese life were found in the novels of U.S. author Pearl S. Buck.

Born Pearl Comfort Sydenstricker in 1892, the daughter of a Presbyterian missionary, Buck grew up in China, where she was tutored by a Confucian scholar named Mr. Kong and was taught English as her second language by her mother. Living in China during the Boxer Rebellion, Buck was profoundly influenced by the anger many Chinese expressed against Western influence.

Buck worked as a missionary in China from 1914 to 1933, before finally purchasing the Green Hills Farm in Bucks County, Pennsylvania, in 1935. Her first novel of Chinese life, *East Wind, West Wind*, was published in 1930, but it was her second book, *The Good Earth*, that would make her name as *the* writer of Chinese life for American readers. The book, still her best-known title, stood on top of the best-seller list for months and won numerous awards, including the William Dean Howells Medal and the Pulitzer Prize. (*The Good Earth* became a best-seller all over again in 2004 when talk-show host Oprah Winfrey selected it for her book club.)

Book after book followed, the majority of which explored the confrontation between East and West as traditional Chinese life faced the challenges of modern times. In 1938, Buck was awarded the Nobel Prize for Literature, becoming the first American woman to win that prestigious award. Buck died in 1973 and was interred at her beloved Green Hills Farm. She designed her tombstone herself, which does not record her name in English. Instead, the grave marker is inscribed with Chinese characters representing the name "Pearl Sydenstricker." To the end, Buck was in many ways as Chinese as she was American.

him, she is unable to adapt to America and gradually sinks into madness. For Kingston, the traits of the "traditional" Chinese woman, feminine and unassertive, were useless—she would have to be strong and brave like her mother to survive in the United States.

Pearl S. Buck's second book, *The Good Earth*, established her reputation as the writer of Chinese life for American audiences. Buck (1892–1973) won the Nobel Prize for Literature, the first American woman to do so.

But in the fifth and final part of the book, "A Song for a Barbarian Reed Pipe," we learn that the details of the confrontation between Moon Orchid and her husband, as presented in the earlier section, may not necessarily be accurate. In this section, Kingston goes on to play with the very act of storytelling, forcing the reader once again to question what is true and what is not. For example, Kingston describes in detail how her mother, in order to help her speak better, cut her frenum (the piece of skin that attaches the tongue to the bottom of the mouth):

> She pushed my tongue up and sliced the frenum. Or maybe she snipped it with a pair of nail scissors. I don't remember her doing it, only her telling me about it. . . . Sometimes I felt very proud that my mother committed such a powerful act upon me. At other times I was terrified—the first thing my mother did when she saw me was to cut my tongue.

Did Brave Orchid actually cut her daughter's tongue? Or, is it a poetic way of describing Kingston's path from silence to speech? Kingston herself does not commit one way or the other, leaving it to the readers to determine what they think happened. For Kingston, ambiguity is at the heart of her storytelling, as she told interviewer Marilyn Yalom in 1980:

> A story changes from telling to telling. It changes according to the needs of the listener, according to the needs of the day, according to the interest of the time. . . . So what happens when you write it down? Writing is so static. The story will remain as printed for the next 200 years, and it's not going to change. That really bothers me, because what would be really neat would be for the words to change on the page every time, but they can't.

So the way I tried to solve this problem was to keep ambiguity in the writing all the time.

By keeping her stories ambiguous or open to argument, their meaning can change with each reading and with each reader.

FINDING AN AUDIENCE

It took Maxine Hong Kingston two years to write *The Woman Warrior*. She then faced a dilemma: Should she publish the book, and if so, how could she get it published?

After all, her book opens with the words, "You must not tell anyone what I am about to tell you." How then could she justify telling everyone about the secrets she was told not to tell? She explained in an interview with Kay Bonetti:

> The wonderful thing about writing is that you can weasel your way around it, because you can think to yourself, "Okay, I'm just gonna write it down. I'm not going to publish it. I'm not going to show it to anybody." Or, you can say, "I'm not telling it, I'm writing it." Then, step by step, you break the silence because there are all these intermediary decisions you can make. At a certain point, by the time I'd written it down, it didn't seem like such a big deal to get it printed.

Kingston knew she had written a good book, one that she wanted other people to read. She also knew that it would not be an easy book to get published. How could the book be categorized? Was it autobiography? Was it history? Was it fiction? (Kingston initially thought of the work as a novel because of the fictional techniques she used in the narrative.) She was also an unknown writer who had written a book that would seemingly appeal only to a small audience of Chinese-American readers.

How could she get it published? (Uncertain if she would ever be able to get it published, Kingston was fully prepared to leave the manuscript in a drawer for history to discover.)

Not knowing much about the publishing industry, Kingston decided to find an agent, someone whose job it was to know publishers and know how to sell a manuscript to the *right* publisher. Her idea was that, if her book was turned down by a major publisher, the agent would then be able to sell the book to a minor publisher, perhaps one in England, Hong Kong, or Canada.

Fortunately for Kingston, getting the book published turned out to be a snap. She easily found an agent to represent her, and remarkably for a first-time author, her manuscript was quickly picked up by Vintage Books. Despite her hopes and dreams, Kingston could little have imagined the extent to which her life would change when her book, now titled by the publisher as *The Woman Warrior: Memoirs of a Girlhood Among Ghosts*, was published in 1976.

6

A Change of Perspective

Although the title that the publisher decided on for her first book was *The Woman Warrior: Memoirs of a Girlhood Among Ghosts*, Maxine Hong Kingston was not particularly happy about it. Her original title was *Gold Mountain Stories*, which the publisher felt sounded like a collection of short stories. Publishers in general prefer not to put out such collections—preferring nonfiction, which is usually easier to sell. But, as Kingston said in an interview with Jody Hoy in 1986:

> I wasn't that happy with either of those titles. I think that calling the book *The Woman Warrior* emphasizes "warrior." I'm not really telling the story of war. I want to be a pacifist. So I keep hoping we will all take the woman warrior in another sense, that there are other ways to fight wars than with swords.

Despite her unhappiness with the title, Kingston could have been only thrilled by the critical and popular response to her first book. Critics fell over themselves in praise for Kingston and her book, which, coming from a previously unknown writer, broke new ground in American literature and established Kingston as one of the country's best writers. Writing in *The New York Times*, influential book critic John Leonard compared her favorably to the top male writers of the time:

> Those rumbles you hear on the horizon are the big guns of autumn lining up, the howitzers of Vonnegut and Updike and Cheever and Mailer, the books that will be making loud noises for the next several months. But listen: this week a remarkable book has been quietly published; it is one of the best I've read for years.

The review made Kingston's name. The book, whose first printing was a mere 5,000 copies, became a national best seller, ultimately selling more than 40,000 copies in hardcover. Other critics agreed with Leonard about the book's exceptional quality, with Sara Blackburn writing in *Ms.* magazine that, in *The Woman Warrior*:

> Maxine Hong Kingston illuminates the experience of everyone who has felt the terror of being an emotional outsider. . . . What is in store for those who read . . . is not only the essence of the immigrant experience— here Chinese, and uniquely fascinating for that—but a marvelous glimpse into the real life of a woman in the family, a perception-expanding report for the archives of human experience. Praise to Maxine Hong Kingston for distilling it and writing it all down for us.

Kingston was named the winner of the 1976 National Book Critics' Circle Award for nonfiction. For a first-time author, indeed, even for the most established of authors, it was an extraordinary honor.

Kingston's editor, Charles Elliott, described in a telephone interview with Karen Horton his worries about how the shy author would handle the pressure of the awards ceremony. He need not have worried.

> She was one of the last of the four main speakers, the previous being [novelist] John Gardner, [poet] Elizabeth Bishop, and [child psychologist and author] Bruno Bettelheim. She arrived wearing a dress that came down all the way to the ground and wearing a lei of flowers that were very fragrant. I don't remember what they were.
>
> She was so short that she couldn't see over the rostrum and had to bend the microphone over the side to speak. I remember thinking, "Oh, no!" She started off with this little tiny voice and before I could believe it, she had it right under absolute control with everyone nearly weeping.
>
> She told the audience that she had been writing for 30 years but never knew she was a writer. "Now you have told me I'm a writer," she said.

Just three years later, *Time* magazine named *The Woman Warrior* one of the 10 best nonfiction books of the decade.

Somewhat surprisingly, despite the media attention and a flood of letters from fans of the book, Kingston was largely unfazed by her new fame and popularity (although she was forced to get an unlisted telephone number, due to the number of calls she received from fans who wanted to talk to her about her book). Indeed, she was not even particularly surprised by the acclaim that her book had received, as she explained to interviewer Karen Horton in 1979:

Maxine Hong Kingston's first book, *The Woman Warrior*, became a national best seller and earned glowing reviews from influential book critics. The book earned Kingston, shown here in a 1977 photograph, the 1976 National Book Critics' Circle Award for nonfiction.

I think I was sort of matter-of-fact about it. Maybe it's because I'm older. Maybe if I were in my 20s, I would be surprised and react to it more violently. I think it made a big difference having a lot of acclaim in my 30s. . . . But I think when you are older, you're sort of set in the way you react to the world. I think I'm pretty much formed. I don't think it's important getting all that attention. Just every once in a while, it hits me.

Now that Kingston was an award-winning, best-selling writer, however, she faced a new challenge. What would she do for her second book?

A DIFFERENT POINT OF VIEW

Fortunately for her, the second book was already partially written. Her original intent with *The Woman Warrior* had been to write a more massive book, one that would tell the story of the men *and* the women who came to America as well as of the land they left behind. During the writing process, as so often happens, Kingston's original intent changed, as she told Eric J. Schroeder in 1996:

At one point, all those stories from *The Woman Warrior* and *China Men* were coming to me at the same time. But later, when I had written down a lot of the stories, I saw they actually could be organized into two different books because the history actually takes place at different times and different places. The women were in China and had their own society. The men were sailing or traveling and were in Chinatowns, and that was another society. Their stories just fell into two different books.

As is generally the case with Kingston, her starting point as a writer was visual, even though a book is made up of words.

Early on in the creative process, she kept envisioning a white triangle, even though she did not know what it meant or how to use it. Finally, though, it struck her. She remembered that her father, telling her stories when she was a little girl, talked about his experience as a stowaway on a boat from Cuba to New York. He hid from the boat's guards in a crate. While in the crate, he could only see through a small crack, and the one thing he often saw through that crack was the triangle of a sailor's white pant legs. She told Paul Skenazy in 1989 that "as a painter, all I would do is draw the triangle, but as a writer, I get to talk about how he came from China and got to Cuba—the story part."

Interestingly, because one book is about women and the other is about men, each book uses myths in a completely different way. Kingston believes that the women's way with a myth differed from that of the men; this, in turn, affected the form of each book. As she explained to interviewer Eric J. Schroeder in 1996:

> The women's myths were more intertwined and in-side their lives. In *The Woman Warrior*, myths and the psyche of the women are integrated. In *China Men* the myths are separate from the men's lives. I'll tell a myth such as a myth about a peacemaker, which is an ancient story. And then that would be juxtaposed with a story about the Vietnam War. The characters in the Vietnam War story are not thinking about the peacemaker myth. I'm asking the reader to read these stories separately, and then to think, "What does this myth have to do with this story? And are these heroes at all affected by this myth? Do they even know about it?" The reader has to struggle with the question of what the ancient myths have to do with our modern lives. . . . So in structuring *China Men*, I keep the myth

and those present-day stories separate, whereas in *The Woman Warrior*, the myths are inside the women and the women are aware of them and living them out.

In *China Men*, the narrative voice is different as well. Like many first works, *The Woman Warrior* was mostly written in the first person—told from the "I" point of view. As Kingston grew and developed as a writer, she began to realize that writing strictly from that perspective could be a weakness, as she explained to interviewer William Satake Blauvelt in 1989:

> At a certain point in my 30s, I began to see this as a personal and artistic shortcoming. I thought there was something really wrong if I can't even use other pronouns . . . and get myself into the point of view of other people.
>
> I struggled with that toward the end of *Woman Warrior*. . . . *China Men* was really supposed to be about those men, but I could only approach it from the "I" again. But as the years went by writing *China Men*, I see that the "I" began to fade away and in the end she [the narrator] becomes a listener. Those men are very much presented as themselves.

It is fascinating to note that even an award-winning, best-selling writer still has to struggle and work on the nuts and bolts of her craft, always trying to work out the best way to tell the story to her reader.

Kingston had to work hard, not only to capture the third-person narrative voice, but to get to a place where she could write about men sympathetically enough. So, to gain an appreciation for the physicality of men, she tested herself physically while writing the book, using a ball-peen hammer and an ax to feel the muscles used in physical labor. By the end of the process, she was proud to be able to write the men's story as she wanted it told, as she knew it *needed* to be told.

It is also fascinating to note that the inspiration, in part, for *China Men* was one of Kingston's favorite books from college, William Carlos Williams's rhapsody of American history, *In the American Grain*. Upon rereading the book, she once again noted that, while the book ends with the Civil War, American history does not end there—*In the American Grain* needed a second volume. *China Men* would be that second volume—an impressionistic look at American history from the perspective of Chinese immigrants, which picks up at the time when *In the American Grain* ends.

CHINA MEN

Like *The Woman Warrior*, *China Men* is divided into interlocking stories: "The Father from China," "The Great Grandfather of the Sandalwood Mountains," "The Grandfather of the Sierra Nevada Mountains," "The Making of More Americans," "The American Father," and "The Brother in Vietnam." Each section of the book ends with a telling of one or two short stories based on traditional Chinese myths and legends. By using this narrative technique, Kingston is able to force the reader to contemplate the ways in which myth and tradition affect and reflect modern reality.

The book's first section, "The Father from China," opens with Kingston looking at her father, a man of few words, a man who almost always refuses to talk about China and his past. Kingston decides that, if he won't tell his stories, "I'll tell you what I suppose from your silences and few words, and you can tell me that I'm mistaken. You'll just have to speak up with the real stories if I've got you wrong."

The section continues with Kingston's partly factual, partly imagined recounting of her father's early life in China. She tells of his own father's attempt, while he was a newborn baby, to trade him for the daughter he had always wanted. She relates his love of studying, his education, his life as a scholar and a teacher, and his marriage to Brave Orchid. She continues with his decision to go to Gold Mountain to make his fortune. Of this, Kingston acknowledges that her father never told her the full story of how he came to America, so she must invent the story as it *might* have happened, offering the reader several possibilities.

Kingston concludes this section by describing her father's life in New York, working in the laundry that he owned with three friends. She tells of his success, of his ability to bring his wife to New York after a 15-year separation, of his being cheated out of his laundry, and of his decision to take his wife to live in Stockton, California.

The second section, "The Great Grandfather of the Sandalwood Mountains," begins in the present, with Kingston discussing her experience of sending money to relatives in China and of her desire to visit the country of her ancestors. "I want to talk to Cantonese, who have always been revolutionaries, nonconformists, people with fabulous imaginations, people who invented the Gold Mountain. I want to discern what makes people go West and turn into Americans. I want to compare China, a country I made up, with what country is really out there." (Even though Kingston had written two books about China at this point in her literary career, she had never visited the country.)

This section continues by telling the story of Kingston's great-grandfather, Bak Goong, who traveled to Hawaii (the Sandalwood Mountains). She re-creates, by combining what is known and what she imagines, his three years of harsh work clearing away the land for the establishment of a sugar plantation.

In the third section, "The Grandfather of the Sierra Nevada Mountains," we learn the story of Kingston's paternal grandfather, Ah Goong, and his three trips to America to work on the building of the railroads. Kingston describes in vivid detail the back-breaking labor of taking down trees, building bridges, filling in ravines, and digging tunnels through the Sierra Nevada Mountains. Many of the Chinese workers, Kingston noted, died forgotten and unknown. "They lost count of the number dead; there is no record of how many died building the railroad. Or maybe it was demons doing the counting and chinamen not worth counting." After work on the railroad is finished, Ah Goong wanders the country, avoiding

THE FIRST TRANSCONTINENTAL RAILROAD

Like many Chinese immigrants to the United States in the middle of the nineteenth century, Maxine Hong Kingston's ancestors worked on the construction of the first transcontinental railroad, which linked the Atlantic and Pacific coasts by rail for the first time. Opened on May 10, 1869, with the driving of the "Last Spike" at Promontory Summit, Utah, the railroad established a mechanized transportation network that made possible the rapid growth of the population and economy of the American West.

Kingston's grandfather, like most Chinese immigrants, worked on the Central Pacific Railroad's portion of the track, which started in Sacramento, California, and traveled 690 miles (1,110 kilometers) through California and Nevada, before connecting with the Union Pacific line at Promontory Summit. Initially, the Chinese were thought to be too weak or fragile to do that kind of hard physical labor. After the first few days, however, the decision was made to hire as many Chinese as could be found in California—and many more were imported from China for the purpose of "working on the railroad."

Work began on January 8, 1863. Great progress was made as the tracks were laid through the Sacramento Valley, but work soon slowed, first by the foothills of the Sierra Nevada and then by the anti-Chinese mob violence and lynching, before returning home to China.

The next section, "The Laws," is a bit of an oddity. In it, Kingston presents a straightforward historical account of the anti-Chinese laws that seemed to allow the racism that Ah Goong tried so hard to escape. Why did Kingston break up her narrative with a lesson in American history? She knew readers would be angry to learn the true history of legal discrimination against the Chinese in America, but why do it in such a factual way?

mountains themselves. Building tunnels through the mountains was difficult and dangerous work, as the Central Pacific began to use newly invented and incredibly unstable nitroglycerin explosives, which sped up both the rate of construction and the death rate of laborers.

Appalled by their losses, the Central Pacific began to use more stable explosives and developed a method of placing the explosives in which the Chinese blasters worked from large suspended baskets that were quickly pulled to safety after the fuses were lit. While most of the men who worked for the Central Pacific received $1 to $3 per day, Chinese laborers who did the most dangerous work received much less. Eventually, they went on strike and received a small increase in salary but still received far less than the non-Asian workers.

Upon its completion, the railroad was recognized as the greatest American technological feat of the nineteenth century. It served as a link for trade, commerce, and travel that joined the eastern and western halves of the late-nineteenth-century United States. Forgotten, though, in the feeling of accomplishment were the laborers who made it possible, including the untold number of Chinese immigrants who died helping to unite the United States.

Maxine Hong Kingston's grandfather came to the United States three times to work on the building of the railroads. Here, some Chinese workers are among those shown at a rail project around 1875. Despite their contributions to the development of the country, the immigrants faced hostility and an array of anti-Chinese laws.

She did it, in part, because she knew that most Americans were unaware of this aspect of U.S. history. Given that, where could she put the information? In an appendix or an introduction? No, she thought, readers would just skip over it there. Footnotes? No, too scholarly. The only way she could think of to present the information needed to understand what her grandfather and so many other Chinese immigrants went through was to put it smack dab in the middle of the book, assuming, rightly so, that readers would be less likely to skip over it.

The book's following section, "The Making of More Americans," returns to the "ghosts" of the previous book. This time, though, the ghosts are not the unknowable white Americans— they are ghosts of a Chinese past, reminders of the China they left behind. In one story, Sahm Goong, one of Kingston's older ancestors called a "grandfather," is haunted by the ghost of his brother, Say Goong. The haunting stops when Sahm Goong orders his brother to return home to China. "It's time to go home then," said Sahm Goong. ". . . Go home! It's time for you to go home now. What's the use of staying here any more? You don't belong here. There's nothing for you to do here. Go home. Go back to China go."

In a similar vein, Kingston tells the story of Sahm Goong's grandson. He has been successfully living in America for many years but is constantly reminded of his past life in China by letters from his mother, urging him to come home and marry a second wife. The grandson ignores the letters, which become increasingly more demanding, begging for money and food and telling him of the famine and hunger ravaging the country.

When the grandson's mother dies, her ghost continues to haunt him, blaming him for her death and tormenting him for ignoring her pleas for help. It is only after the grandson returns to China to bring his mother's ghost back home to her grave and to perform all the proper religious rites that he is able to return home to live in peace. Was there a real ghost? Was it simply the grandson's guilty conscience? In telling the story, does it really matter?

In the final two sections, "The American Father" and "The Brother in Vietnam," Kingston returns to a more realistic narrative. In "The American Father," she tells again of her father, relating the facts as she knows them about his move to Stockton, his work at the gambling house, and finally, the opening of his own laundry.

"The Brother in Vietnam" is an expression of Kingston's own pacifism and disgust of war. She tells of growing up during World War II and watching newsreels showing the atrocities performed by the Japanese against American soldiers and Chinese civilians. The images she saw horrified her so much that her mother was forced to take her out of the movie. "You cried so much that the usher ghost threw me out of the theatre," Kingston's mother tells her years later.

Kingston points out that many Chinese men came to the United States to avoid being forced to serve in the Chinese military: "The Gold Mountain does not make war, is not invaded, and has no draft. The government does not capture men and boys and send them to war." Although her father was able to avoid the draft, her brother, forced to decide between going to Vietnam or running away to Canada, enlisted in the Navy, under the assumption that there he would have the least chance of having to actually kill anybody. The book ends with the short tale "On Listening," which recounts the numerous versions of the Gold Mountain legend that Kingston hears at a party, suggesting, as does the book as a whole, that there are as many versions of the Chinese immigrant experience in America as there are tellers of the tales.

REACTION AND AWARDS

China Men was published in 1980 to the same sort of rave reviews that *The Woman Warrior* had received four years earlier. Author Edmund White, writing in *The Washington Post*, said:

> By delving into her own girlhood memories, by listening to the tall tales her Chinese immigrant

parents told her . . . by researching the past in books and by daydreaming her way into other lives, the author has stitched together a unique document so brightly colored that it seems to be embroidery sewn in brilliant silk threads, a picture of fabulous dragons sinuously coiling around real people, a mandarin square of triumph and privation, of memorable fact and still more vivid fancy. . . . [Kingston has] freely woven fairy tales into her recital of facts and rendered her account magical.

In a 1991 interview with Donna Perry, Kingston elaborated on the way that *China Men* intertwines the real and the imaginary:

I hear about those people from my mother. I met most of those men, but not all of them. But they were still a real presence. I never met my grandmother either, but they were [all] so real that I know, through my mother's stories, that they existed in real life. So they exist in my imagination. In fiction, there are people I think about and I hear their voices, and then they are embodied in people who walk up to me and say things that are lines, exactly as I need. So the line between imagination and reality is not a sharp one.

She talked about this even further in an interview with Eric J. Schroeder in 1996:

I think that having two categories—fiction and non-fiction—is too small. I picture a border between fiction and nonfiction, and I am making that border

(continues on page 90)

Being Asian American

FINDING THE ASIAN-AMERICAN VOICE

The work of Maxine Hong Kingston is infused with the meaning of what is to be an Asian American. Her books examine the roles of immigrant Chinese men and women in American life, examine the lives of their children and the conflicts between the generations, and look at the ways that both generations' Chinese past influenced their lives in America. By using Chinese history and myth, combined with elements of autobiography and fictional techniques, Kingston has given readers a unique perspective on the Asian-American influence.

There have been some who have disagreed with the way that Kingston used traditional Chinese myths and legends, and most of these critics were, perhaps surprisingly, fellow Asian Americans. Writer Frank Chin, in particular, objected to Kingston's use of Chinese legend and myth and the way that she modernized and transformed traditional Chinese stories to tell her own story. In his essay, "Come All Ye Asian Writers of the Real and the Fake," Chin wrote of Kingston (along with fellow writers Amy Tan and David Henry Hwang) that they:

> . . . are the first writers of any race, and certainly the first writers of Asian ancestry, to so boldly fake the best-known works from the most universally known body of Asian literature and lore in history. And to legitimize their faking, they have to fake all of Asian American history and literature, and argue that the immigrants who settled and established Chinese America lost touch with Chinese culture, and that a faulty memory combined with new experience produced new versions of these traditional stories. This version of history is their contribution to the stereotype.

To make his point, though, Chin often misreads Kingston's intentions. He attacks, for example, Kingston's retelling of the Fa Mu
Lan story—in particular, Kingston's changing of the story so that
the history of Mu Lan's village is tattooed onto her back, an event
"borrowed" from the story of the male Chinese hero Yüch Fei. Chin
argues that Kingston does this to emphasize the cruel treatment
of women in traditional Chinese society. Kingston, on the other
hand, argues that she did it to give the *strength* of men's stories
to women.

Chin, a traditionalist, cannot bear to see any alteration in the
way that Chinese legends and stories were told, and he resents
Kingston's usurpation of these stories to tell the stories *she*
wants to tell about the Asian-American experience. To Kingston's Asian-American critics, her responsibility as a Chinese-
American writer is to be true to the Chinese community as *they*
see it. For her part, Kingston sees herself as a voice that is both
of the Chinese-American community and uniquely her own—free
to use the stories as she wishes. As she told interviewer Karen
Amano:

> I saw myself as finding and creating my own individual voice,
> but at the same time it is also the voice of Asian-American
> people. It's also the voice of all those people such as the No
> Name Aunt. This is a person with no voice. She died a long
> time ago without a voice, and I, through my own voice, can
> give her one. I can give voice to people who have no political
> voice, who have no personal voice; it's possible to give them
> a voice through my own work. So it is both individual and it's
> a universal or racial voice.

(continued from page 87)

very wide; fiction is a narrow place on one side, and nonfiction is a narrow place on another side, and there's this great big border in the middle, in which real life is taking place and also fantasies and dreams and visions.

Kingston believes that, in *The Woman Warrior* and in *China Men*, she has, indeed, written a new kind of biography. They are different, she feels, because she tells "the biographies of imaginative people. I tell the imaginative lives and the dreams and the fictions of real people. These are the stories of storytellers, and so instead of telling the dates when people are born and where they're born, I tell you what their dreams are and what stories they tell." By continuing and transforming the "talk-stories" of her childhood, Kingston had created a new kind of literature.

China Men also went on to be a best seller. It received the 1980 National Book Award for nonfiction. It was also nominated for a National Book Critics Circle Award and was a finalist for the Pulitzer Prize in nonfiction. At the same time, the Bancroft Library at the University of California, Berkeley, began to collect Kingston's papers as one of its special collections.

Perhaps the most interesting award recognition that Kingston received was from her home state of Hawaii. A Buddhist sect based in Honolulu named her a Living Treasure of Hawaii during a chant- and incense-filled ceremony at Hoopa Hongwanji Temple. Kingston was only 39, particularly young to have received the honor (in Japan, the honoree has to be at least 80 years old), and she was Hawaii's first Chinese-American Living Treasure. Kingston was both touched and overwhelmed to receive the recognition, telling Timothy Pfaff that:

Hawaii has all kinds of traditions and ceremonies that are not immediately apparent. I didn't know about this one until I was made a part of it. This tradition comes from ancient China via modern Japan. In the same way that we designate paintings and monuments and mountains as treasures, they designate certain people as Living Treasures. During the ceremony, the Buddhist priests talked about their own experience of coming to Hawaii and wanting to be a part of its culture. They decided that one way was to honor some of Hawaii's treasures. It makes me feel really good to be honored by them. It feels as if the islands are saying, "You can be a part of Hawaii, too."

Undoubtedly, though, the reaction to *China Men* that touched Kingston the most was that of her father, who had dreamed of being a poet when he was a young man. When Tom Hong read a pirated Hong Kong edition of the book, he made notes as he read—responses, corrections, additions. (As Kingston had asked him to in the book itself, "You can tell me that I'm mistaken. You'll just have to speak up with the real stories if I've got you wrong.") For a man so often silent, it was his way of communicating with his daughter.

Later, the book with Hong's additions was put on display with some of his daughter's papers at the Bancroft Library. Kingston took her father to the exhibit and showed him "their" book, open to a page with many of his beautifully handwritten notes. Her father was completely happy at seeing his words on display along with his daughter's, and he turned to others in the crowd, proudly saying in English, "My writing, my writing." You can only imagine the emotions that Maxine Hong Kingston was feeling at that moment.

Of course, just because Kingston's work has generally received high praise does not mean that she has not had her critics. Some have faulted her for not remaining true to the traditional, classical versions of Chinese legends. To this, Kingston responds that she feels no need to remain "true" to the classical versions. If legends are to stay alive, she feels, they must change to reflect new realities. In addition, Kingston is quick to point out that her versions of the classical tales come not from "high" Chinese culture but from the traditions of the poor, working-class people of the region in southern China that was home to her family.

Even so, despite the criticism, with two books, two best sellers, and a number of major awards under her belt, Maxine Hong Kingston had established herself as one of America's most interesting and innovative writers. Once again, she faced the challenge that all writers face—what would she do next?

7

Trying Something New

I'm going to take a little time off and act like a regular person. I've told all my childhood stories that I wanted to tell, and I don't have any more stories accumulated. Now I have nothing, but I feel good about that, too. I feel like I am looking out over an ocean. It's a blank ocean, and the sky is empty too. I'm watching to see what comes up over the horizon, and that is going to be the next book. I'm going to make something out of nothing, which is the greatest creativity. And I'm willing to wait a long time.

—Maxine Hong Kingston,
in an interview with Timothy Pfaff

It would be nine years between the publication of *China Men* and her next book. In the meantime, Kingston did, indeed, act like a regular person.

This period was a time of major changes in her personal life. Starting in 1977, Kingston had been a visiting professor of English at the University of Hawaii, Honolulu. In 1981, she resigned her post. It had been a busy four years, and she wanted to relax a bit and have as normal a life as possible.

Part of having as normal a life as possible meant purchasing, for the first time, a home for her and her family. She had always been proud to be a renter, with the freedom to be able to pick up her belongings and move whenever she felt the desire to do so. Now, she was a homeowner, someone who was, as she described in the essay "Our First House," "one incarnation from snail or turtle or kangaroo."

Of course, Kingston did not buy the house to become a traditional housewife. As she wrote in *Hawai'i One Summer*, "I had never become a housewife. I didn't need to own land to belong on this planet." What the house, surrounded by lush tropical plants and two ponds, provided her with was a writer's garret—a room just under the pitched roof of a house, usually the attic. In "Our First House," she lovingly described it as:

> . . . a writer's garret, the very writer's garret of your imagination, bookshelves along an entire wall and a window overlooking plumeria in bloom and the ponds. If I could see through the foliage, I could look downhill and see the (restored) hut where Robert Louis Stevenson wrote his Hawai'i works.

For the woman who as a child had to clear away space in her parents' storeroom to write in, the ability to have what British author Virginia Woolf called "A Room of One's Own" was perhaps one of the most satisfying rewards of her success as a writer.

Kingston took the opportunity, now that she was between books, to spend time with her family, especially her son Joseph Lawrence, who was a teenager and a Hawaiian in ways his parents would never be. She also traveled, touring Japan, Australia, Indonesia, Malaysia, and Hong Kong. The trip, which was

JUDGING LITERATURE

While Maxine Hong Kingston's books have received countless prizes, she had the opportunity while in Australia to bestow some literary prizes on others. The setting for the awards, though, was somewhat surprising.

In Australian pubs, there is a popular game known as Writers Sports. There is a row of typewriters, and writers, after a considerable amount of drinking, are asked to write three-minute poems, which are then judged. Kingston was asked to judge a game of Writers Sport in a different setting—with an audience of 1,000 people, spotlights like at a boxing match, and four typewriters in a row waiting to be used. There was even an MC, like a sports announcer, who gave running commentary as the participants composed their poems.

There were several contests. In one, the poets pulled a slip of paper from a hat, each with a different genre or type of poetry. In another contest, audience members yelled out suggestions for character names or a last line for the poem, with the poets having to write a poem leading up to that line. For Kingston, judging the competition was tough, especially given the difficulty of understanding the often thick Australian accents. At one point, Kingston gave a high number of points to a poem that had a line that she *thought* was "The koala bear was eating aphrodisiac gumbies"— she was particularly taken by the creation of the word *gumbies*. Unfortunately, Kingston later learned that the poet had said *gum leaves* not *gumbies*. Still, Kingston was so taken by the idea of this sort of literary competition that she considered ways to use it in her classes—without the alcohol, of course!

sponsored by the United States International Communication Agency and the Adelaide Festival of Arts in Australia, gave Kingston her first opportunity for foreign travel, and it served merely to whet her appetite for more. The opportunity would come in 1984, when Kingston had the chance to visit the land she had written about but had never seen, the land of her ancestors and the source of inspiration for her first two books. Kingston would be going to the People's Republic of China.

HOW WOULD IT COMPARE?

It was a trip she had long contemplated but delayed for several reasons. First, she had wanted to finish her first two books, knowing that the reality of China might conflict with the imaginary China that she wrote about. Second, for years, her parents had warned her about making such a trip. They were concerned that something bad would happen if she went. Since so many of her family members had been killed in the revolution, her parents thought she might be killed as well. As the 1970s turned into the 1980s, however, and as China opened up to the West and more and more people were able to travel there, Kingston knew that the time had come for her to go.

She would not be traveling on her own. The 1984 trip, sponsored by the University of California, Los Angeles, and the Chinese Writers Association, was designed to introduce some of the United States's greatest authors to Chinese writers, poets, and scholars. It was an eclectic mix to say the least; the group included Native American novelist Leslie Marmon Silko, African American novelist Toni Morrison, and gay American poet Allen Ginsberg.

For Kingston, the trip was an amazing experience. She was finally seeing the country she had heard about her whole life. She was seeing the places she had only seen in her imagination, and it was fascinating if scary to compare the China she had written about with the China she was seeing. What if she had gotten it wrong in her books?

She hadn't. Somewhat to her surprise, her imagination had captured the reality perfectly. As she said in an interview with Paula Rabinowitz, "The colors, and the smells, the faces, the

In 1984, Maxine Hong Kingston finally visited the People's Republic of China, as part of a group of U.S. writers meeting their Chinese counterparts. Among the others in the contingent was Toni Morrison *(above)*, the prize-winning author of *Song of Solomon* and *Beloved*.

incidents, were much as I had imagined. Many people said to me, 'Welcome home.' I did feel that I was going back to a place I had never been."

Even visiting her family's village, she was struck by how often what she had written corresponded to what she was seeing. Not only that, what she saw also served to corroborate the stories that her mother had been telling her since she was a little girl, as she told Kay Bonetti:

I was so gratified because I saw what I had described, and it felt like I was coming home because I had described it right. Not only that, but it gave me a faith in talk-story because they had described it pretty much the way it looked. But also, there were things that I wish that I had seen earlier so that I could have written it more accurately. [For example,] I saw the Hong family temple, and it's right next to the well where the aunt jumped in. I brought pictures back of the well and of the temple, and then my mother said, "Oh you know, the guys used to stand around the temple on the steps and they used to make comments at the girls that are drawing the water, trying to get them flustered so they'd drop their earthenware jars, and then the men would laugh." And then I thought, "God I wish I'd known that. That would have been perfect to put into the 'No Name Woman' section."

It must have been an overwhelming experience for Kingston to see the spot where her aunt had drowned herself, the aunt that she had rescued from oblivion and returned to the family history.

LEAVING HAWAII

Upon returning home from China, Kingston, after 17 years in Hawaii, moved to Los Angeles, California, so that her actor husband, Earll, would have greater opportunities for work. While she was not unhappy about moving to Los Angeles, one aspect of the change was very upsetting to her. Her son, Joseph Lawrence, now 20 years old, had decided to remain in Hawaii. An aspiring musician, he had lived in Hawaii since he was three years old, and Hawaii was his true home, as Kingston discussed in an interview with Kay Bonetti in 1986:

> I would have really liked to have raised him as a reader, as a more scholarly person, but he's become a Hawaiian. That's what he is now. He's a Hawaiian, and his culture is

Hawaiian music, and he has Hawaiian families that are like his families.

Although Hawaiian, Joseph Lawrence is still very much attached to his Chinese roots. Indeed, like many of his ancestors, he has seen his own ghosts and spirits—but instead of being Chinese ghosts and spirits, they are Hawaiian.

A NEW BOOK

The change of scenery gave Kingston the impetus to complete a book that she had been working on for several years. The book, *Tripmaster Monkey: His Fake Book*, was her first novel, her first work of complete imagination.

Kingston loved the challenge. Writing a novel gave her the chance to invent everything within the book, freeing her as a writer. Yet it was a more difficult book to write because, as she said to Jody Hoy, "I could keep inventing this world forever." Indeed, at one point, the book was more than 1,000 pages long, and Kingston feared that she would never finish it.

It was not just the freedom to invent that excited Kingston—it was the freedom to use language that excited her as well. In her first two books, Kingston had felt the pressure of having to translate a foreign culture, its words, history, and myths, to a non-Asian audience. She explained to Paul Skenazy that she wanted to "use everything I know, to use the language at the hardest level that I can work it, the American language, that language that I hear and speak. In *The Woman Warrior* and *China Men*, I kept putting it aside." With *Tripmaster*, though, "it was like, oh, I'm going to be free. I'm going to put anything I want in this. . . . I'm just going to play with all the books that I read and it felt to me like an outpouring of things that I had been holding back and denying."

(continues on page 102)

Other Notable Individuals

AMY TAN

After the publication of Maxine Hong Kingston's best-known works, *The Woman Warrior: Memoirs of a Girlhood Among Ghosts* and *China Men*, the door was opened for a new generation of Asian-American writers, writers whom *Entertainment Weekly* described as "The Children of 'Woman Warrior.' " Among the best known and most popular of these is the Chinese-American author Amy Tan.

Tan was born in 1952 in Oakland, California, the daughter of Chinese immigrants. Her father, John Tan, was an electrical engineer and Baptist minister who came to the United States to escape the chaos of the Chinese Civil War in the late 1940s. Her mother, Daisy, had divorced an abusive husband in China while losing custody of her three daughters. She was forced to leave them behind when she escaped China just before the Communist takeover in 1949.

Amy's father and her oldest brother both died of brain tumors within a year of each other while Amy was still a child. Mrs. Tan moved her surviving children to Switzerland, where Amy finished high school. By this time, Amy and her mother were barely speaking to each other. Their conflict only increased when Amy left the Baptist college her mother had selected for her to follow her boyfriend to San Jose City College.

Tan further angered her mother when (in a manner similar to Kingston) she abandoned the pre-med courses her mother had urged her to take so that she could take the courses *she* wanted: English and linguistics. After receiving her bachelor's and master's degrees in these fields, Tan, who had married her boyfriend, lawyer Louis DeMattei, settled into a job as a language-development consultant and directed a training project for developmentally disabled children.

She also started a business-writing firm, writing speeches for salesmen and executives. While doing well financially, she soon found herself dissatisfied with her work. She studied jazz piano to satisfy her

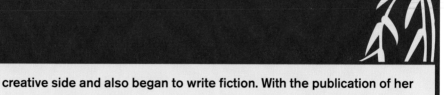

creative side and also began to write fiction. With the publication of her stories, Tan began to consider the possibility of becoming a full-time writer of fiction.

Just as she was embarking on this new career, Tan's mother fell ill. Tan promised herself that, if her mother survived, she would take her to China to see the daughters she had left behind nearly 40 years earlier. When Mrs. Tan regained her health, the two went to China. The trip was an extraordinary one for Tan, allowing her to gain a new perspective on her often difficult relationship with her mother. Upon returning to the United States, she set to work on a new book in earnest.

That novel, *The Joy Luck Club*, earned rave reviews upon its publication in 1989 and sat on the *New York Times* best-seller list for more than eight months. The book has been translated into 17 languages, including Chinese. Other books, all best sellers, have followed, including the novels *The Kitchen God's Wife*, *The Hundred Secret Senses*, *The Bonesetter's Daughter*, and *Saved Fish from Drowning*, as well as the children's books *The Moon Lady* and *The Chinese Siamese Cat*. She has even written the libretto (otherwise known as the words or text) for an opera based on *The Bonesetter's Daughter*.

In all of these works, Tan, like Kingston, examines the relationship between mothers and daughters and between the older generation of Chinese immigrants and their more "American" children. Her essays and short stories have appeared in hundreds of anthologies and textbooks, and her work is assigned as "required reading" in high schools and universities around the world. She has even appeared on the animated TV series *The Simpsons* as herself, perhaps the ultimate compliment of one's pop-culture renown. If Maxine Hong Kingston made Amy Tan's work possible, it will be interesting for all readers, given Tan's great popularity, to see what writers emerge inspired by her work.

(continued from page 99)

The book is set in Berkeley, 1963, a time and place that Kingston was quite familiar with. Indeed, Kingston was able to draw on her own experiences in writing the novel, which also uses Chinese legend as a counterpoint throughout the narrative.

The "monkey" in the title is Wittman Ah Sing, Chinese American, and a recent graduate of Berkeley. Ah Sing, whose name is a tip of the hat to American poet Walt Whitman, is a tall, skinny poet/playwright/rebel. As described by Kingston to Jody Hoy:

> It's about a young, hip Chinese-American man who has the spirit of the trickster monkey. He has to solve all kinds of problems about who he is, and how he will make a living, and how he will be an artist, and how he will be a Chinese American.

What is a trickster monkey? In Chinese legend, there is Sun Wukong, the Monkey King, a combination saint and trouble-maker, not unlike Wittman Ah Sing. Wittman's dream, similar to Kingston's, is to write and stage an enormous play, com-bining and interweaving classic Chinese novels, legends, and folktales into something so large that it will change the lives of everyone who sees it.

In her use of the Monkey King, Kingston united his spirit with what she saw as the spirit of the 1960s. In her view, the monkey was an underdog, without a lot of power, who often had to resort to trickery to achieve his goals. "He has to think of new ways to change things. I even think of Martin Luther King, when he thought of those demonstrations, nonviolent acts, new acts in order to change the world. To me, that is evidence that the monkey was here," she said in an interview with William Satake Blauvelt.

In 1989, the year this photograph was taken, Maxine Hong Kingston published her first novel, *Tripmaster Monkey: His Fake Book*. Although the book got mixed reviews, *Tripmaster Monkey* was a success, and Kingston went on to receive several awards.

Once again, Kingston found a way to use Chinese legends to enhance and deepen the meanings of her work. But, instead of telling her own story, she was telling someone else's story, with a narrative voice that is again in the third person. Although it is a work of fiction, Kingston uses stories from her own time at Berkeley. A major scene, for instance, involving a party and poetry reading is taken from Kingston's life, albeit indirectly. Kingston told interviewer Marilyn Chin in 1983 that, while in the process of writing the book, "I'm writing a party scene that takes place one Saturday night, but in this party I've used the 50 most interesting parties I've been to in 20 years." In this way, everyday life is transformed into art.

Once again, Kingston found a way to allow for ambiguity in her art. She alludes to this in the book's subtitle: *His Fake Book*. What, after all, is a fake book? Kingston defined it and how it relates to her book in a 1989 interview with Blauvelt:

> This is a jazz term. Jazz musicians used to compile a book of basic tunes, songs, chords. Sometimes it would be just the beginning of a tune, then they would improvise. So I was trying to write a prose book with basic plots, suggestions for social action, for trips. I hope to trip the reader out and have them improvise further.

In other words, what readers bring to the book is as important as what the writer provides. Kingston's goal is to throw out a few things for readers and let them improvise like a jazz musician and finish the book in their own minds.

The book, published in 1989, is obviously a challenging one and not for every reader. Reviews were mixed, with some critics praising the book's narrative energy and complexity and others complaining that the book was overwritten and even tedious. Where many critics, positive and negative alike, agreed was on the character of Wittman, who often came across as tiresome, obnoxious, and frankly unlikable.

Interestingly, many critics drew parallels between the character of Wittman and that of Kingston's harshest critic, her old college acquaintance Frank Chin, who was also an English major at Berkeley at the same time. Was this her way of getting back at Chin for his criticisms of her work? Kingston denied this, telling Blauvelt:

> I actually don't believe in revenge. I see this book as a kind of big love letter. If it is answering—if it is—then it's like him sending me hate mail, and I send him love letters, it's like that. I sure hope his soul is big enough to understand that.

Despite the mixed reviews, *Tripmaster Monkey: His Fake Book* was a popular success and went on to win the P.E.N. USA West Award for fiction. Other awards for Kingston followed, including the California Governor's Award for the Arts, the Brandeis University National Women's Committee's Major Book Collection Award, and the American Academy and Institute of Arts and Letters Award in Literature.

Kingston also decided in 1990 to accept an invitation to return to her alma mater, the University of California, Berkeley, as a Chancellor's Distinguished Professor of English. As she and Earll settled into their new home in the Oakland Hills, Kingston began to work on what she planned as her next book, to be titled *The Fourth Book of Peace*, and contemplated her good fortune. Little did she know that, in the following year, two events would combine to make 1991 one of the most difficult and traumatic years of her life.

8

Making
a Difference

The first blow occurred in September 1991, when Maxine Hong Kingston's father, Tom Hong, died in Stockton. For Kingston, whose relationship with her father had only strengthened over the years, it was a painful loss.

One month later, Kingston was again in Stockton, attending the religious ceremonies surrounding the one-month anniversary of her father's death. Driving home to Oakland that afternoon, she heard over the radio that fires had broken out in the Oakland Hills. The first reports placed the fires far enough away from her house that she was not too concerned. The closer she got to Oakland, however, the closer the news reports said the fires were to her neighborhood. By the time she was in Oakland, reports were saying that 150 houses had burned and that an area next to her house was on fire. Panicked, Kingston drove as close to her house as she could. There, she saw that "ashes were falling and the sun was all red."

The police had blocked the road leading to her house, but as soon as the police were distracted, Kingston set out on foot to her house. Conditions were just too bad for her to continue, and she was forced to come back. Not willing to give up, she tried another route, but it was no use. Although she got within a block of her house, wires were down, smoke was everywhere, and Kingston realized that her house was gone. Destroyed along with her house were all of her possessions, including family heirlooms, mementos, and, perhaps most immediately upsetting, the only manuscript of her work-in-progress *The Fourth Book of Peace*. Everything was gone.

But, while standing there devastated in the smoking ruins of what was once her neighborhood, something wonderful happened, as she described to Joan Smith:

> Two men came up on bicycles and I said, "I just lost my novel," and one of them patted me on the head and said, "It's up here and you're still alive," and the other said, "Would you like a ride on my handlebars?" What a blessing, what a blessing, [Kingston thought]. . . . Down the hill through this incredible wind, with logs and fires and fire houses, watching the flames go up all around and the ashes falling. It really taught me to live in the present because I was *really enjoying* that ride.

Even so, 156 pages of her manuscript, equaling years of hard work, were gone forever. Coincidentally, as Kingston pointed out to Smith, "In ancient Chinese mythology there were three books of peace and they were burned, in wars or fires or book burnings, so it's right on a kind of cosmic level that a fire came and burned my book, too. It feels as if I am working with the forces of destruction and creation, so I am going to do it again."

And being a writer, that's what she did. Kingston, for whom writing is as essential as breathing or eating, really had no other choice. She would start again. From scratch.

Only one house remained standing in this neighborhood in the Oakland Hills after a fire in October 1991 that destroyed nearly 3,000 homes. Maxine Hong Kingston's house was among those lost in the fire. Besides her possessions, the fire also claimed the only copy of her work-in-progress, *The Fourth Book of Peace*.

REWARDS AND GIVING BACK

Kingston was given a financial and moral boost in 1992, when she received a fellowship from the Lila Wallace Reader's Digest Fund. Instead of using the money for herself, she used it to help a group of people who had been a concern of hers since the 1960s—Vietnam War veterans.

She had had the idea of holding writing workshops for veterans for many years, ever since attending a retreat organized by the Vietnamese Buddhist monk Thich Nhat-Hanh entitled "Healing the Wounds of War." At the retreat, American and Vietnamese war veterans came together for meditation and discussion, but it occurred to Kingston that one thing was missing from the retreat—art. On the last day of the retreat, she held a writing workshop on her own; so upon receiving the Wallace fellowship money, she knew what she wanted to do.

Kingston organized a series of workshops to be held on a regular basis, open to veterans of all wars. The workshops were Kingston's way of helping those whose lives were damaged by war, a way to bring together a community of writers to heal one another and to create art. Kingston described a typical day's workshop in a 1996 interview with Eric J. Schroeder:

> We usually tried to meet in a beautiful place, like a farmhouse, or some lovely place in nature. We would begin the day with meditation, and then we'd usually have some kind of an exercise or question that we'd all think about; each of us would then talk about ourselves in relation to some question, such as how we felt on Veterans Day . . . I usually give a talk on some aspect of writing, and then everybody goes to some nice corner of the room and we write together. . . . When we're writing together, in community, I like to think that we're not writing alone. We know there's other people who want to hear our stories. Then we eat together. . . . After

lunch I evoke the Bodhisattva of compassionate listening, Kuan Yin, the goddess of mercy. Then we read our work aloud and listen to one another. We all try to listen with compassionate understanding and without judgment. We listen for what is said, but also what's not said.

LOST BOOKS

While the loss of the manuscript for Maxine Hong Kingston's *Fourth Book of Peace* in a fire was a tragedy, she is not alone as a writer in suffering that kind of loss. Throughout time, many potentially great books have been lost or destroyed before publication.

The memoirs of the English poet George Gordon, Lord Byron, were destroyed by his publisher and biographer on the grounds that they were too "scandalous" for readers of the time. The same fate occurred to the unpublished memoirs of the English writer and explorer Sir Richard Burton, whose manuscript was destroyed by his wife, Isabel, in an effort to save their reputations from scandal.

But perhaps the most famous example of a destroyed manuscript occurred to the British historian Thomas Carlyle. In 1835, he loaned the first part of the manuscript for his book *The French Revolution: A History* to his friend, the philosopher John Stuart Mill, for comments and advice. Mill, in turn, loaned the manuscript to his lady friend, Harriet Taylor. Unfortunately for Carlyle, Taylor's maid mistook the manuscript for scrap paper and used it to start a fire in the fireplace—all but the first two pages were destroyed.

Imagine having to explain to your friend that the only copy of his handwritten manuscript (typewriters were still to be invented) had been destroyed. Fortunately for Mill, Carlyle forgave him and quickly went to work rewriting his book, which was published just two years later. Like Kingston, Carlyle had refused to let his loss devastate him. "My will is not conquered," he said.

Everyone takes a turn reading, and then we do a walking meditation. Next we give responses to one another's
readings, and then we have a meditation again. That's
the end of the day. I like to think that we're living together for one whole day.

Kingston was not only helping to heal the veterans of previous wars; she also spoke out and took a stand against any future
wars. On March 8, 2003, she, along with 26 other protesters, including fellow writer Alice Walker, were arrested after crossing
a police line in front of the White House as they demonstrated
against the possibility of war in Iraq. (The war began nearly two
weeks later, on March 20.) Obviously, Kingston's commitment
to peace had not diminished since her protests against the Vietnam War in the 1960s.

SHE IS A WRITER

Despite or perhaps because of her long-time political activism,
Kingston is, to the very heart of her being, a writer. Not that
writing ever gets easy, even for a renowned and beloved author
such as Maxine Hong Kingston. It's still hard work, and Kingston often puts off the moment that she begins to write: doing
dishes, sharpening pencils, and straightening and restraighten-
ing her desk.

As with many writers, there are times when the inspiration
is not there. Kingston realizes, though, that it will come. All she
needs is patience and the knowledge that there is, in some ways,
an upside to the difficult times, as she hopefully explained to
Karen Horton:

Some days when it's really bad, it's good for you, too. As
long as you feel it's bad, you keep working on it. And you
feel it's bad because you have a kind of vision of what it
should be and so you strive and work and rework. But

Maxine Hong Kingston read from her book *The Fifth Book of Peace* in April 2005 during a 24-hour read-in at a library in Salinas, California. The event was held to help save the public libraries in Salinas. *The Fifth Book of Peace* was published in 2003.

when you feel good, maybe it's very deceptive, because then you don't rework.

But when she does it, she does it; writing, rewriting, and constantly revising her work, up to the moment of publication. Throughout the process, she constantly turns to her most honest critic, her husband, Earll, for advice. When the last draft of a book is completed, when she thinks she has taken it as far as she can, she turns it over to him. He gives her his criticism and feedback, and then, of course, Kingston does one more draft. And one more.

Indeed, it took many years, drafts, and revisions before her next book, *The Fifth Book of Peace*, was ready for publication in 2003. The book, which was reborn from the ashes of her burnt manuscript for *The Fourth Book of Peace*, tells the story of that fire, of her attempts to recreate the manuscript that was lost. It follows her quest to discover the myths surrounding the lost Three Books of Peace; it discusses her work with war veterans to create a literature of peace; and it ends in an epilogue describing her arrest outside the White House in protest of the war in Iraq.

It is, by any definition, an extraordinary work of literature. Classic Kingston, it once again brings together all of her major concerns: war and peace, loss, myth and legend, the need for community, into a kaleidoscopic work of art. *Publishers Weekly* said of it that:

> Kingston writes in a panoply of languages: American, Chinese, poetry, dreams, mythos, song, history, hallucination, meditation, tragedy—are all invoked in this complex stream-of-consciousness memoir. . . . This work illumines one writer's experience of war and remembrance while elevating a personal search to a cosmic quest for truth. This is vintage Kingston: agent provocateur, she once again follows her mother's dictate to "educate the world."

And by educating the world, Kingston has proved herself one of America's great writers, a fact confirmed on November 20, 2008. On that night, at the awards dinner for the National Book Awards, Maxine Hong Kingston was presented with the National Book Foundation's Medal for Distinguished Contribution to American Letters. This award, given to "a person who has enriched our literary heritage over a life of service, or a corpus of work," has been granted to some of America's greatest writers: Joan Didion, Eudora Welty, John Updike, Philip Roth, and Toni Morrison. Kingston was now ranked with America's literary elite. At the award ceremony, she said, "Thank you for accompanying me on the immense journey and thank you for giving me this spurt of praise that will carry me to the finish line."

She is not, though, content to rest on her considerable laurels. Kingston is now in the process of completing work on a

In November 2008, the National Book Foundation presented Maxine Hong Kingston with its Medal for Distinguished Contribution to American Letters. She plans her next work to be a book-length poem.

book-length poem; she has written eloquently about Barack Obama in Hawaii; and she continues to speak about the issues she cares most about: war, peace, feminism, community, and the healing power of art. As an Asian American, she has opened the door for a whole new generation of writers. Authors Amy Tan, Gish Jen, and a host of others, all, in some part, owe their careers to Maxine Hong Kingston.

Her books, especially *The Woman Warrior* and *China Men*, are still widely read and studied. The Modern Language Association, for example, has reported that *The Woman Warrior* is the most widely taught text in modern university education. Demonstrating the book's complexity and near encyclopedic range and depth, it is taught not just in literature classes, but also in anthropology, Asian studies, composition, education, psychology, sociology, and women's studies courses.

As a writer and an activist, Kingston has held onto her pacifist beliefs and has persisted in using the power of her art to spread her message of peace, as she does in the last paragraphs of *The Fifth Book of Peace*:

> The images of peace are ephemeral. The language of peace is subtle. The reasons for peace, the definitions of peace, the very idea of peace have to be invented, and invented again.
>
> Children, everybody, here's what to do during war: In a time of destruction, create something. A poem. A parade. A friendship.
>
> A community. A place that is the commons. A school. A vow. A moral principle. One peaceful moment.

Maxine Hong Kingston's distinctive literary voice is one to read, to contemplate, to treasure. She is not only a Hawaiian "Living Treasure." She is one of America's living treasures as well.

CHRONOLOGY

1940   Born on October 27 in Stockton, California.

1955   Publishes her first essay, "I Am an American," in *American Girl* magazine.

1962   Graduates from the University of California, Berkeley, with a B.A. in English; marries Earll Kingston, an aspiring actor and classmate at Berkeley.

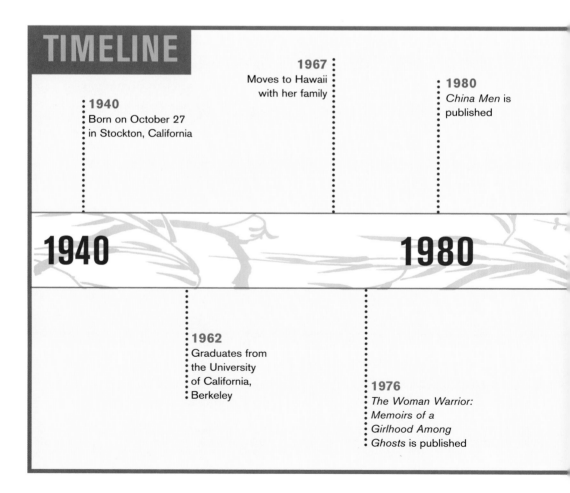

TIMELINE

1967
Moves to Hawaii
with her family

1980
China Men is
published

1940
Born on October 27
in Stockton, California

1940

1980

1962
Graduates from
the University
of California,
Berkeley

1976
*The Woman Warrior:
Memoirs of a
Girlhood Among
Ghosts* is published

1964 The Kingstons' son, Joseph Lawrence Chung Mei, is born.

1965 Earns teaching certificate and begins to teach high school.

1967 Moves to Hawaii.

1976 Her first book, *The Woman Warrior: Memoirs of a Girlhood Among Ghosts*, is published; it wins the National Book Critics' Circle Award for nonfiction.

1980 *China Men* is published; it wins the National Book Award for nonfiction; a Buddhist sect names Kingston a Living Treasure of Hawaii.

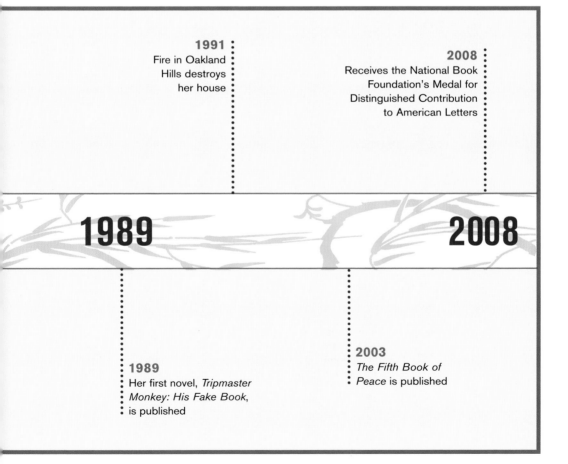

1991
Fire in Oakland Hills destroys her house

2008
Receives the National Book Foundation's Medal for Distinguished Contribution to American Letters

1989

2008

1989
Her first novel, *Tripmaster Monkey: His Fake Book*, is published

2003
The Fifth Book of Peace is published

1981 Receives Guggenheim Fellowship.

1984 Visits the People's Republic of China for the first time; moves with her husband to Los Angeles.

1989 Her first novel, *Tripmaster Monkey: His Fake Book*, is published; it wins the P.E.N. USA West Award for fiction.

1990 Begins to teach at the University of California, Berkeley; moves with her husband to Oakland Hills.

1991 Fire in Oakland Hills destroys Kingston's house and all of her belongings, including the only copy of her work-in-progress, *The Fourth Book of Peace*.

1992 Begins to hold writing workshops for war veterans.

2003 *The Fifth Book of Peace* is published.

2008 Receives the National Book Foundation's Medal for Distinguished Contribution to American Letters.

GLOSSARY

ambiguity—Uncertainty.

AWOL—Absent without leave, or absent without permission.

Communism—A political ideology that promotes the establishment of an egalitarian society based on common ownership of goods as well as control of property and the means of production.

conscription—A draft.

constitution—The basic principles and laws of a nation that determine the powers and duties of the government and guarantee certain rights to the people.

discrimination—The unfair treatment of a person or a group because of prejudice.

domino theory—A theory that, if one nation becomes Communist-controlled, the neighboring nations will also become Communist-controlled.

draft—Compulsory enrollment in the armed forces.

draft dodger—Someone who is drafted into the military and refuses to serve.

first person—A way of storytelling in which the narrator appears as the "I," recollecting his or her part in the events related, either as a witness of the action or as an important participant in it.

ghetto—A section of a city occupied by a minority group that lives there especially because of social, economic, or legal pressure.

Gulf of Tonkin Resolution—The resolution, passed in 1964, gave the U.S. president authorization for the use of military force in Southeast Asia, without a formal declaration of war by Congress.

hieroglyph—Picture symbols used in a writing system.

ideograph—A graphic character that indicates the meaning of that character without indicating the sounds used to say it.

immigration—The act of coming to a foreign country to settle there.

libretto—The text of a dramatic musical work, such as an opera.

myth—A traditional story of ostensibly historical events that serves to unfold part of the worldview of a people or explain a practice, belief, or natural phenomenon.

pacifist—A person who is strongly and actively opposed to conflict, especially war.

phonetic—Of or relating to spoken language or speech sounds.

pictograph—A picture representing a word or an idea.

plumeria—Frangipani, which are shrubs or small trees of the dogbane family that are native to the American tropics and are widely cultivated as ornamental plants.

prejudice—An irrational attitude of hostility directed against an individual, a group, a race, or their supposed characteristics.

rebellion—Open, armed, and organized resistance to a constituted government.

sovereignty—The authority of a state to govern another state.

stream of consciousness—A literary technique that presents the thoughts and feelings of a character as they occur.

teach-in—An extended meeting usually held on a college campus for lectures, debates, and discussions to raise awareness of or express a position on a social or a political issue.

third person—A method of storytelling in which the focal character or characters are referred to as "she," "he," "it," or "they," but never as "I" or "we" (first person) or as "you" (second person).

treaty—A formal agreement between two or more nations, as in reference to terms of peace or trade.

BIBLIOGRAPHY

Alegre, Miel, and Dave Weich. "Maxine Hong Kingston After the Fire." Powell's Books, December 3, 2003. Available online at http://www.powells.com/authors/kingston.html.

Blackburn, Sara. "Notes of a Chinese Daughter." *Ms. Magazine*, January 1977.

Buckmaster, Henrietta. "China Men Portrayed with Magic." *The Christian Science Monitor*, August 11, 1980.

"'Color Purple' Author, 26 Others Arrested at Peace Rally." CNN, March 9, 2003. Available online at http://www.cnn.com/2003/US/03/08/sprj.irq.war.rallies/index.html.

Feng, Pin-chia. "Maxine Hong Kingston." Available online at http://www.cc.nctu.edu.tw/~pcfeng/CALF/ch1.htm.

Grice, Helena. *Maxine Hong Kingston: Contemporary World Writers*. Manchester, England: Manchester University Press, 2006.

Jordan, Tina. "The Children of 'Women Warrior.'" *Entertainment Weekly*, June 21, 1991. Available online at http://www.ew.com/ew/article/0,,314696,00.html.

Kingston, Maxine Hong. *Everyman's Library: The Woman Warrior* and *China Men*. New York: Alfred A. Knopf, 2005.

———. *Hawai'i One Summer*. Honolulu, Hawaii: University of Hawai'i Press, 1998.

———. *The Fifth Book of Peace*. New York: Vintage International, 2004.

———. *Tripmaster Monkey: His Fake Book*. New York: Alfred A. Knopf, 1989.

Madsen, Deborah L. *Literary Masters: Maxine Hong Kingston*. Farmington Hills, Mich.: A Manly Inc. Book, The Gale Group, 2000.

Martin, Michel. "Maxine Hong Kingston Takes Pride in Mixed Heritage." NPR, July 4, 2007. Available online at http://www.npr.org/templates/story/story.php?storyId=11732740.

"Maxine Hong Kingston." Available online at http://www.uncp.edu/home/canada/work/canam/kingston.htm.

"Maxine Hong Kingston." Available online at http://voices.cla. umn.edu/vg/Bios/entries/kingston_maxine_hong.html.

"Maxine Hong Kingston Biography." Available online at http:// www.bookrags.com/biography/maxine-hong-kingston-dtx.

"Maxine Hong Kingston Biography." Available online at http:// www.bookrags.com/biography/maxine-hong-kingston-aya/.

Ono, Kent A. *A Companion to Asian American Studies*. Maiden, Mass.: Blackwell Publishing, 2005.

"Review of *The Fifth Book of Peace*." From *Publishers Weekly*. Available online at http://www.amazon.com/Fifth-Book-Peace-Maxine-Kingston/dp/0679440755.

Simmons, Diane. *Maxine Hong Kingston: Twayne's United States Authors Series*. New York: Twayne Publishers, 1999.

Skenazy, Paul, and Tera Martin, editors. *Conversations with Maxine Hong Kingston*. Jackson, Miss.: University Press of Mississippi, 1998.

Xi, Xu. "Maxine Hong Kingston." *Time*, November 5, 2006. Available online at http://www.time.com/time/asia/2006/ heroes/at_kingston.html.

FURTHER RESOURCES

BOOKS

Carpenter, Frances, and Malthe Hasselriis. *Tales of a Chinese Grandmother: 30 Traditional Tales from China*. North Clarendon, Vt.: Tuttle Publishing, 2001.

Chang, Pang-Mei Natasha. *Bound Feet & Western Dress: A Memoir*. New York: Anchor Books, 1997.

Chin, Frank. *Donald Duk*. Minneapolis, Minn.: Coffee House Press, 1991.

Genthe, Arnold, and John Kuo Wei Tchen. *Genthe's Photographs of San Francisco's Old Chinatown*. Mineola, N.Y.: Dover Publications, 1984.

Kwong, Peter, and Dusanka Miscevic. *Chinese Americans: The Immigrant Experience*. Westport, Conn.: Hugh Lauter Levin Associates, 2000.

See, Lisa. *On Gold Mountain: The Hundred Year Odyssey of My Chinese-American Family*. New York: Vintage, 1996.

Wong, Jade Snow. *Fifth Chinese Daughter*. Seattle, Wash.: University of Washington Press, 1989.

WEB SITES

Bill Moyers Journal: Maxine Hong Kingston
http://www.pbs.org/moyers/journal/05252007/profile.html

Chinese-American Contribution to the Transcontinental Railroad
http://cprr.org/Museum/Chinese.html

Chinese Immigration to the United States, 1851–1900
http://lcweb2.loc.gov/learn/features/timeline/riseind/chinimms/chinimms.html

INDEX

PHOTO CREDITS

ABOUT THE AUTHOR

DENNIS ABRAMS attended Antioch College, where he majored in English and communications. A voracious reader since the age of three, Dennis is a freelance writer who has written numerous books for young-adult readers, including biographies of Hamid Karzai, Ty Cobb, Anthony Horowitz, Xerxes, Rachael Ray, and Hillary Rodham Clinton. He lives in Houston, Texas, along with his partner of 20 years, two cats, and their dog, Junie B.